THE WARRIOR WITHIN ME

The Real Secret

ISSA E. NESHEIWAT

- A Promise Made In Solidarity
- Sacred Vow
- That Became A Mission

Based on a True Story

THE WARRIOR WITHIN ME:
The Real Secret

A RESCUE OF FAITH + A PROMISE MADE IN SOLIDARITY
+ A SACRED VOW THAT BECAME A MISSION

BASED ON A TRUE STORY

ISSA E. NESHEIWAT

Charleston, SC
www.PalmettoPublishing.com

The Warrior within Me

Copyright © 2020 by Issa Nesheiwat

First Edition

Hardcover ISBN: 978-1-64111-730-2

Paperback ISBN: 978-1-64990-468-3

eBook ISBN: 978-1-64990-739-4

TABLE OF CONTENTS

"Surely goodness and mercy shall follow me all the days of my life, and I shall dwell in the house of the Lord forever." **(Psalms 23:6)**

To my eldest son, it is because of you that I made this vow to God. My testimony, and the lesson I was taught, I share because of the night I dropped to my knees and swore an oath to write about the victory. God has truly delivered his end of the promise, now I deliver mine.

FOREWORD

I HAVE KNOWN ISSA FOR about seven years, which puts us at about the time this story began. I first knew him as a real property renovator and landlord through my job. And now, since he asked me to assist him in editing this book, I know him as a devoted believer, one who has been at war, like so many of us, with the truth about whether God is really there. And I know him as a friend.

Issa has written a thought-provoking book about his fight for his spirituality, and how he came to be a 110% believer in the Lord, Our God and Jesus Christ, Our Savior ... The Father, The Son and the Holy Ghost. It is about his war with his trust and faith and how God and Christ saved him.

I have been an agnostic for my entire life. I have even had many friends who were believers, including my husband, and none of them were able to make me question MY beliefs in this way! I was convinced that believing in something I could not see was ignorant. But during the time I have spent with Issa, my belief system has been turned upside down. Every doubt I have ever had is followed by a huge question mark. I am now wondering about searching for answers.

Once you have read this book, you will really want to put your questions to the test. His experiences will make your eyes spring open, and you will want to believe that his story is true. I believe that everything in this story is exactly what happened to my friend.

Through this book, Issa will make you want to know all about his story and to question what you have doubted. It is his hope and mine that you, the reader, will be unable to put this book down until the very end. Then, we hope that you will be so taken with what has happened to Issa, that you will want to work more toward your love for all that is The Warrior Within You.

Nancy L. Beatty-Griffin

PREFACE

THE WARRIOR WITHIN ME IS based on real events that took place in my life, a storm that raged within my soul. However, these events are examples of my fight through spiritual warfare, which I had to engage in, or else lose my most prized possessions. I have traveled on this road called faith for years now, and through the process I was taught how to wage war when the fight came to me, and win it. I have become anchored in my faith, as it guides me every day. I write this book to tell you my story and from it, I hope to answer some of your questions about how faith works, explain the force behind the fight we all face every day, and give you a guide through all that I did from the trials I endured. I will reveal to you the importance of holding on to faith in God, in the most difficult and uncertain of times, times when it seems that He's not there. My goal is to inspire the nonbeliever to seek our Lord Jesus and give a deeper insight of spiritual warfare to the believer. We owe it to ourselves to find the truth in God.

INTRODUCTION

EVERYONE WONDERS AT A POINT in their life if God can truly talk to them in a dream, if miracles are capable of happening, and if God is real. If these things are true, how can I draw near to the Creator, and gain access to this supernatural power? Are the keys to victory in my life's battles from health, family, marriage, depression, and business won through spiritual warfare?

The answer to all these questions is yes. You can unlock the door to victory in all these different areas of your life, and more.

However, the problem with many people not winning the fight in the battlefield of life is simply spiritual! They don't understand how the invisible struggle between good and evil actually work. We do not have any self-thought; every thought we get is influenced by either God or the enemy. When we act on these thoughts, whether pro or con, we engage the force within the spiritual realm. We cannot trust ourselves because we are emotional beings, and our mind and flesh are naturally of this three-dimensional world.

> *"THE[1] heart is deceitful above all things, and desperately wicked;*
> *Who can know it?"*
> ***(Jeremiah 17:9)***

This idea of God and the devil - angels and demons - is scary to many, including myself at first. However, you need to understand that you don't go into war without having a four-star general lead you and without all the proper weaponry and gear to protect yourself and loved ones. Once you're properly lead and equipped, you will ultimately win the good fight of faith in your life. The four-star general who took me through my battles was Jesus Christ, and the weapons and gear He equipped me with were the sword of the spirit, the helmet of salvation, the breastplate of righteousness, the shield of faith, the belt of truth, and the shoes of the gospel of peace. There you go! That's exactly what you need to win and overcome every time. How do I know this you ask? Because He told me:

> *"FOR though we walk in the flesh, we do not war according to the*
> *flesh. For the weapons of our warfare are not carnal but mighty in God*

---

1   The first word of every bible verse has been capitalized for emphasis.

for pulling down strongholds, casting down arguments and every high

thing that exalts itself against the knowledge of God, bringing every

thought into captivity to the obedience of Christ...."

(2 Corinthians 10:3-5)

But please keep an open mind and understand that everything has opposites. The opposite of light is dark, the opposite of positive is negative, the opposite of hot is cold, and the opposite of God is evil. Also, there are repercussions to our actions from the physical world we exist in, which directly affect and alter what happens in the spiritual realm. This chain of actions changes outcomes we see manifest in our lives. According to Newton's[2] Third Law, for every action there is an equal and opposite reaction.

"BE not deceived; God is not mocked: for whatsoever a man sows, that

shall he also reap.

For he that sows to his flesh shall of the flesh reap corruption; but he

that sows to the Spirit shall of the Spirit reap everlasting life."

(Galatians 6:7-8)

---

2   Newton invented calculus and the theory of gravity.

You don't have to be a superhero who wears a cape and fights off demons after leaving the office; the contrary is true. I went through seven years of battles and experienced things for which many people would have simply given up on God! Where many would say God is not real, and if He is, why am I going through this again, and again, and again, I held on to my faith and always remembered to hold God accountable to His word. He cannot lie. He is perfect. A couple of scriptures that I always recite to myself are:

"BE strong and of a good courage, do not fear nor be afraid of them; for the Lord your God, he is the one who goes with you. He will not leave you nor forsake you". **(Deuteronomy 31:6)**

"BEING confident of this very thing, that He who has begun a good work in you will complete it until the day of Jesus Christ"
(Philippians 4:6)

I'm just a child of God who refused to stop trusting Him and believed the Living Word with all my heart. I also put on the full armor of God and allowed myself to be guided by the Holy Spirit. Although I wrestled with God and questioned His work at times, I still refused to give up on Him as He never gave up on me. That's how I won every battle!

The supernatural world is another realm and does not confide to the laws of this world we physically exist in. This book will give you the key to unlock the mystery of winning in all the affairs of life whether big or small. You will understand a dimension that is very difficult to comprehend and will be encouraged to open your spiritual eyes. I struggled with this for years, until I reached the point I'm at now. I'm a man who has experienced a series of trials, visions, dreams, and answered prayers all my life and explicitly for the seven-year cluster of trials which began in 2013 and ended in 2020 (and as I write this book). I would like to share the story of my battles to inspire you to seek God, to hold on to Him during turbulent times, to look at a situation whether good or bad from a different lens, and to never lose hope because nothing is what it seems. The victory was given to us over two thousand years ago when Jesus Christ was crucified for our sins and rose from the dead on the third day -- when he trampled upon death and gave us the victory. Knowing and believing this fact changes everything in the spiritual realm and the outcome that you get in the world that you understand.

People from throughout my community would come up to me for years and ask me how I survived? And how am I so strong? And "I wish I had your strength" and on and on they went. Although they were amazed, many of them completely lacked understanding of what was actually taking place right before their eyes. If they could look at me through spiritual eyes, they would see a man covered with battle wounds and scars. Although they have healed, they have left marks that will never be removed.

Nonetheless, I would try to explain it. But who are we kidding here, how do you explain this topic in a short and casual conversation. Yet, I tried, and several friends and family who took interest in the matter started their journey in trusting God and they never looked back. I guess they felt if God was with me through my turbulent times, as he empowered me and gave me victory, He would also give them the victories over their battles and struggles as well. Although I was being tried and going through Hell - if I may say it like that - I was inspiring people and giving them hope to have faith and to hold on to that faith as they trust the God they couldn't see.

The gain here is very simple: it's to have faith that could move mountains and win in all the affairs of life no matter what obstacles are thrown at you. My hope is for you to lose all your fears and trust God with absolute certainty. I have extracted these biblical principles and Godly instructions and put them all together for you in a comprehensive manner. This should be more than enough reason to read this book in its entirety. I will tell you my story in a timeline of dreams that I had throughout the years and the correlating events that took place shortly thereafter or before. Through my life's events, you will see how the Holy Spirit lead and taught me everything I know. I got on my knees and promised God a long time ago that if He would turn my storms into a testimony, then

I would tell my story of His Majesty to the world. In the same fashion, I now make a promise to you that you'll have better insight and understanding in the spiritual realm that exists and dictates our lives, if we let it. You will understand the raging war that never stops between good and evil. I also assure you that growth in your faith and encouragement from God will be gained from my testimony.

Remember: What a man sows he reaps. We must take accountability for our actions! We sometimes create our own demise and after we have reaped our rewards, we blame God for our troubles. We come with an instruction manual called the Bible. Yet most of us avoid reading the manual that is made for us from the One who created us. He would know His creation better than we could ever understand ourselves.

This influences our end-result in the physical realm. Everything that happens to us, first happens in the spiritual realm that hovers over us. But most of us go around feeling helpless, alone, depressed, and defeated with no means of fighting or changing an outcome and, in the process, accepting the situation as it is. But I have news for you my friends! You can change the outcome and have control over the invisible that influences your life.

It is crucial that you do not skip chapters in this book. You must read the book in its entirety to understand the process that brings out The Warrior Within You. This wisdom is worth its weight in gold. So, let those who have eyes see and those who have ears hear.

CHAPTER 1

-Reading the Bible

I was sitting in my bedroom crossing my legs over one another on my bed. I was looking at myself from an aerial view. I saw my head planted into the Bible as I was reading aloud in Aramaic, strolling my fingers from right to left as I was construing the text in a convincing tone. I kept laser focus on the book before me and understood every word that came out of my mouth. It made sense as I continued to read along.

I WOKE UP COMPLETELY TAKEN by this dream. I didn't have the slightest clue of what I read and why I was reading the Holy scriptures in a language that is completely foreign to me. What was more baffling was the fact that I was **seven years old**! I remember feeling touched by something special and excited about it. I ran to my mother and told her what I had just dreamt about and asked her what she thought the meaning behind it was. She smiled at me with a fascinated look as I rambled on about what

I had just seen myself do in this dream. I continued to pry her for the meaning and all she kept on telling me was that "it was a good dream", until she finally found an excuse to walk away from me. She needed to escape all the questions that she couldn't answer. I would be lying if I told you that she didn't have a puzzled look on her face, that was filled with a sense of intrigue as she went along with her motherly duties. At seven years old, I did not think much of it after that day. I never forgot that dream; it was etched into my mind and soul forever. Until this day, I wonder what from the Bible I was reading. Perhaps God will reveal it to me one day.

I grew up in south Yonkers, New York, a fairly large city with a closely knit Jordanian community within a melting pot of ethnicities. I was raised in a Christian household with my parents, brother and three sisters. I was the lucky one because I was the eldest out of the pack. Now, being the oldest has its privileges, but also comes with challenges that may not affect the younger siblings to the same extent. Being the first-born son to immigrant Jordanian parents came with tons of pressure. I was my father's protégé.

At the time, I thought I had the toughest dad in the world. All he wanted me to do was go to school, study, do my homework, get the best grades, and do it all over again until I became a doctor or a lawyer. I didn't understand why it was so important for him that I did one of these professions. Now that I'm a proud father of four beautiful children, I totally understand his motives. He wanted me to have a better life than he had, filled with prestige and financial freedom and not to struggle like he did.

I always assumed the responsibility of taking care of my younger siblings and family. This responsible nature and caretaker behavior came naturally since it was imbedded within me growing up. I remember my parents leaving us home alone and I would take charge immediately. I would go around the apartment, locking all the doors and windows, and making sure our home was secure. I would be very watchful over my younger brother and sisters. Protecting my loved ones was never an option; it was within my most inner core to do just that. You can say I'm wired like a guard dog, and could be relentless in keeping the ones I care for safe from harm. It is because of this very same warrior spirit that God entrusted me with, that I endured relentless trials that came when I got older. God knew that I wouldn't stop fighting. In my youth, I always walked around feeling like I was the alpha-dog everywhere I went. What I thought to be tough was actually the warrior spirit yet to be controlled and tamed by God.

Inexplicable dreams have always been a part of my life, even from early on. I grew up like any other child and had the same interests as all my friends. I didn't necessarily stand out because of my dream encounters. I ignored them and went about my day and childhood not thinking twice about them. However, I never forgot the visions that came to me.

Now as I speak to you, it all makes sense: These dreams were not only messages from God, but also a timeline of my life to be shared with you and to give you understanding on a relationship I have with God; to show you how I fought the good fight, how God never left me, how He taught me to war in this invisible realm, and in the hopes to inspire you to seek Him.

Another time God spoke to me in my adolescent years was in the following dream.

-Picking Up Everyone's Cross

At the age of 8, I was walking up Oak Street, a street I grew up on in Yonkers, New York, a very urban neighborhood. As I was walking up the hill by the old bodega just two city blocks from my house, I found green and orange crucifixes tossed out on the sidewalk. I knelt over and picked them all up, about ten or so. I remember feeling a strong sense of righteous anger and insult as I started bashing the people that threw them out. I thought, who would do such a thing? I was in such a hurry to get them off the ground as I shoved them in my pocket.

Reflecting back now, it feels like God was telling me that I will be picking up my cross and following Him. I was also going to carry more than just one cross. I would be picking up the cross for my family as well in a series of trials that were yet to come. That's not how I interpreted it at the time. Actually, I remember dwelling on that dream for several days after I had it, then shrugging it off like the rest. I really didn't have the mental capacity to reflect on the deeper meanings back then. My main focus was negotiating with my dad to stay up late on school nights and playing with my friends.

God has been communicating to us in dreams and visions since the beginning of time. This is mentioned numerous times in the scriptures and as we look at the book of Job and Joel we can start to unfold one of God's favorite methods to interconnect with us.

"FOR God speaks in one way, and in two, though man does not perceive it. In a dream, in a vision of the night, when deep sleep falls on men, while they slumber on their beds, then he opens the ears of men and terrifies them with warnings, that he may turn man aside from his deed and conceal pride from a man; he keeps back his soul from the pit, his life from perishing by the sword". **(Job 33:14-18)**

"AND it shall come to pass afterward, that I will pour out my Spirit on all flesh; your sons and your daughters shall prophesy, your old men shall dream dreams, and your young men shall see visions". **(Joel 2:28)**

The Lord spoke to all the great prophets of the Bible through dreams starting with Abram, who later was renamed Abraham. In Genesis, God gave Abraham a vision and made a covenant with him:

"AFTER this, the word of the Lord came to Abram in a vision: 'Do not be afraid, Abram. I am your shield, your very great reward.'"
(Genesis 15:1)

God promised Abraham a son at a very old age and to make Abraham the father of a great people. He said that Abraham and his descendants must obey Him. In return God would guide them and protect them and give them the land of Israel.

One of the best ways for God to communicate with us is during our sleep. When we have fallen asleep, our bodies are completely detached from our conscious minds and we enter into an altered state within our subconscious. Sleep is another state of comatose, but with a different kind of brain activity. Dreams come upon us during the deepest part of our sleep called Rapid Eye Movement or an REM state and our subconscious mind starts to reveal things to us. This is when we are most vulnerable physically and spiritually. Things that don't normally make sense in our waking life, all of the sudden make sense in our dreams. This state of mind is when God can talk to you without you disrupting the message with your conscious mind. We have a tendency to overthink things and try to use our "intelligence" to interpret meanings and look for solutions that are logical and understood when we are awake in our three dimensional world. We can also dismiss God in our awakened state because of these very reasons. God does not live by the laws that govern our physical world -- He lives outside of them. Remember, we are talking spiritual warfare and we are trying to understand the spiritual realm, not the physical. Although they are interconnected, they operate on different plains.

God can choose to communicate with us any way He wants. The question is, do you know how to listen to Him? Many people make bad decisions, while others make great decisions. One decision, whether good or bad, can change the trajectory of your life forever and impact you and your family for years, if not generations to come. The Holy Spirit can minister to us through the following ways in addition to our dreams.

Firstly, He will give us confirmation to His message. Have you ever noticed the same message would keep popping up in front of you in everything you read, or multiple people, even strangers will give you the same message throughout your day, or all the stations on the radio are talking about the same thing that's been on your mind that day? No matter what, you just can't get away from it. This is a way God gives confirmation or will lead us to something that we aren't seeing. There is a passage in 1Samuel 3:3-10 that shows us how God had to send Samuel confirmation through Eli. God called Samuel out of his sleep three times, and each time he would run over to Eli and ask, did you call me? It wasn't until the third time that Eli realized that it was God calling him and instructed Samuel on what to do the next time he's called.

"AND before the lamp of God went out in the tabernacle of the LORD where the ark of God was, and while Samuel was lying down, that the LORD called Samuel. And he answered, "Here I am!" So he ran to Eli and said, "Here I am, for you called me."

And he said, "I did not call; lie down again." And he went and lay down.

Then the LORD called yet again, "Samuel!"

So Samuel arose and went to Eli, and said, "Here I am, for you called me." He answered, "I did not call, my son; lie down again." (Now Samuel did not yet know the LORD, nor was the word of the LORD yet revealed to him.)

And the LORD called Samuel again the third time. So he arose and went to Eli, and said, "Here I am, for you did call me."

Then Eli perceived that the LORD had called the boy. Therefore, Eli said to Samuel, "Go, lie down; and it shall be, if He calls you, that you must say, 'Speak, LORD, for Your servant hears.'

So Samuel went and lay down in his place.

Now the LORD came and stood and called as at other times, "Samuel! Samuel!"

And Samuel answered, "Speak, for Your servant hears "
(1 Samuel 3:3-10)

Secondly, He will give you inner peace about a decision or situations even when it seems absurd at first. This greater peace that you feel in your heart exceeds any human understanding. Think of a time that you made a decision about something, this could be work related or in any other area of your life. Do you remember a sense of peace about that decision or anxiety? Did you at a later point regret that decision telling yourself "I knew I shouldn't have!" or did you say "thank God I made the right choice!" This is a way God talks to you my friends, so don't dismiss these feelings of intuition because God is also the Holy Spirit. The Spirit of God will communicate in this way with our spirit. He will lead and teach by convicting us or confirming to us.

Thirdly, a message of the Holy Spirit will never contradict the Bible. God's message will always be in absolute harmony with the Holy scriptures. This is how you can discern the spirit message, by seeing if it aligns itself with the word of God.

The spiritual realm can be a very dangerous arena to enter on your own, and I don't recommend you playing with the spirit world that hovers around us without understanding it and having the proper tools in place. Please don't be afraid, this is not meant to discourage you or keep you from tapping into your God-given power and obtain your promised victories. Rather, like anything else in life, you must have understanding and knowledge of how it operates. Believe me when I tell you the enemy is more afraid of you than you are of him. He will try to keep you ignorant and unequipped to defend yourself. Let me try to explain it to you in this short parable.

A prince is born to a very powerful king. This prince is very dear to his father and will inherit the kingdom one day. All the king's people knew this. As a child the prince knew his father was the great king and would go to him and ask for anything he wanted, and it would be done. The king loved his son, the prince, so much that he empowered him to command all the servants and soldiers of the entire kingdom to his every word, and they must obey, because the prince operated under his father's power. The prince grew up knowing the strength that he inherited. He behaved in a way that demonstrated his father's authority that was given to him. After all, he is the prince and his father is the king. Who in the kingdom would challenge that?

Now imagine if the prince is born to the same king who possessed the same power. This time the prince didn't realize who his father really was and the kind of supremacy he had access to through his father. This prince would never go to his father for anything and always strayed away with the henchmen. He would lack the authority to command merely out of unawareness. He would lack the confidence to command in addition to not really having a birth right relationship to the power source. He wouldn't be able to instruct anyone in the kingdom. Not because he has less power, but because he is ignorant to the power he does have. This, in return, would mirror weakness, in that the soldiers and all the king's servants would take advantage of him. They would show him no respect and never obey a command that would come out of his mouth.

In the same way, we must understand that Jesus Christ is our King and Heavenly Father; He has dominion and absolute power over the evil in this world and beyond it. We, as believers, are children of the Most-High King, Jesus. We have been given power and authority over evil through Him. So why wouldn't you take the authority that was given to you? You are all princes and princesses; take hold of your birthright authority.

"BEHOLD, I give unto you power to tread on serpents and scorpions and over all the power of the enemy, and nothing shall by any means hurt you". (Luke 10:19)

I tell you this confidently, God has never lied to me. Not through his word nor through confirmations I received during prayer. It is very important that I emphasize this, because trusting God is hard at times for many people when enduring unpleasant situations. Believe me, this trust I speak about was not easily accepted by me in the beginning. Not because I didn't want to trust God; rather, it's completely against human nature to put a difficult situation into the hands of an invisible being. Trusting God is a form of faith. Faith is the only way to please God. Nothing we can possibly do as sinful people can delight God more than faith that's engaged through trust.

"BUT without faith it is impossible to please him: for he that comes to God must believe that he is, and that he is a rewarder of them that diligently seek him". (Hebrews 11:6)

Trust activates faith, and this moves God on your behalf to war for you and favor you in all the circumstances you may face. God knows our human nature, so don't feel discouraged if you're a believer and still have trust issues with Him. I encourage you to start taking little steps towards entrusting the Almighty and building your trust over time, until you are confident in your faith in God. This can be done with many day-to-day events such as trusting God to aide you in finding the right new car, helping you retain material you've studied for an exam, or providing you with an avenue to pay some bills. The list goes on as I'm sure you can find many little things in your daily life to trust to God. This means you have to look for the new car, study for your exam, and not be lazy to work a little extra. Your efforts will be guided even if it takes time for some things to happen. Don't take delays as a no, it's protection and will happen in the right time and under the will of God. Don't confuse your wants with your needs. God knows the desires of your heart and will give them to you, but he must trust you first. Sometimes getting what you want could be a curse if received too soon. He must lay down the foundations in your relationship with Him in order to anchor and protect you.

I promise you God is patient and when he sees you trying to seek Him, He will help you through His Holy Spirit. We must become like Christ and that means becoming patient when things don't happen on our watch. Throughout your walk with God, you will have the help of the Holy Ghost. This is one of the reasons He had to die, to send us the helper His Holy Spirit.

Faith is a spiritual muscle that needs to be exercised every day. You don't go to the gym once a month and expect to see bigger biceps. People who are in amazing shape live a rigorous lifestyle training and dieting along with many other healthy habits to achieve the body you see on them. In the same fashion you must train your faith for strength and endurance. You must start reading the Bible and listening to the Word as if you are watering a flower to grow.

"SO then faith cometh by hearing, and hearing by the word of God".
(Romans 10:17)

Reading the scriptures is a great form of seeking God. What better place to look for the Creator than in His word? In the Bible, you will learn about God and His nature. You will read about all the prophets' experiences and learn from them. You will also receive direct answers on all issues of life pertaining to how we should live a healthy lifestyle, counseling in many difficult decisions, marriage, raising our children, even what foods to stay away from. This is a very deep well of wisdom as I haven't even scratched the surface here, I assure you that you can never read the word of God just one time and have enough of it. It's called the "Living Word" for a reason, you will always be able to extract new information that was never picked up the first time. The text comes to life and touches your very soul, literally.

God can also be sought through modern day technologies such as the internet and YouTube. Many great teachers and pastors upload sermons and explanations to topics that could be tough to interpret otherwise and answer questions you may have. A couple of people I recommend for you to watch are Dr. Charles Stanley and the late Dr. Ravi Zacharias. I have watched these men preach and explain the gospel in such a profound way which helped me to grow in understanding over the years.

One of my favorite ways of seeking God is good old fashioned prayer. There is nothing like it, the thought of having a conversation with God, as He takes all my needs, worries, and burdens gives me a sense of security and confidence. A relief comes upon me when I am finished, as I know He is the only one who can help me through my dilemmas. There is a peace that comes from this which acts as confirmation to me. The moment I lose anxiety and fear, I know God has stepped into the situation. It is most delightful for me when I feel the spirit of the Lord come upon me. My body fills with unexplainable goosebumps and tears just fall from my eyes. It's peace that cannot be explained, but must be experienced to understand the feeling of relief you get.

*"BE anxious for nothing, but in everything by prayer and supplication, with thanksgiving, let your requests be made known to God; and the peace of God, which surpasses all understanding, will guard your hearts and minds through Christ Jesus". (**Philippians 4:6-7**)*

Prayer needs to be a daily habit. This is not something you do when things are going wrong and cease from it when they start to go well. Keep in mind the enemy will pick up on your patterns and exploit you. Know the enemy's schemes and devices so you are not fooled and attacked without a defense. Praise God always and keep in communion with Him during all the chapters of your life. There is an old saying: "If you only pray when you're in trouble, then you're in trouble." Remember, God says the prayers of a righteous man advances considerably. We must pray always and live as righteously as we can.

Naturally to occur after seeking the Lord in His Word, you begin to become familiar with the text and you will start to remember verses that speak directly to all situations and circumstances you encounter. This is one of the arsenals that is needed; the more ammo you have, the better equipped you are to fight off the attacks of the enemy. The mind is the enemy's playground and what you know or don't know could be the very reason you either win or lose.

The United States military doesn't just have one navy ship, two submarines, and three fighter jets. They have many of each of these and countless other weapons and the soldiers to implement its force on any attack that may come upon our nation. Our military is the strongest in the world for many reasons, and a large count of weaponry is one of them.

When you could retain many verses and/or meanings of these verses, you then become equipped in the word of God, which is the sword of the spirit. This will be your main line of fire against unfavorable situations and/or lies that are being put into your thoughts. I can't tell you how many times I immediately revert back to a scripture that I knew by heart which related to a situation that was unfolding, and immediately exposed it as false and/or rebuked it instantly. Think of this as a fact checker and if it doesn't line up to The Word of God, then it's false and the opposite is true.

The enemy is deceptive and very clever. As we look at the story of when Jesus was tempted in the wilderness, we will start to see how this is displayed. Let's first read the passage, and then I will point out the technique that was used.

"THEN Jesus was led by the Spirit into the wilderness to be tempted by the devil.

After fasting forty days and forty nights, he was hungry.
The tempter came to him and said, **"If you are the Son of God, tell these stones to become bread."**
Jesus answered, **"It is written: 'Man shall not live on bread alone, but on every word that comes from the mouth of God.'"**
Then the devil took him to the holy city and had him stand on the highest point of the temple.

"If you are the Son of God," he said, *"throw yourself down. For it is written: "He will command his angels concerning you, and they will lift you up in their hands, so that you will not strike your foot against a stone."*

Jesus answered him, *"It is also written: 'Do not put the Lord your God to the test."*

Again, the devil took him to a very high mountain and showed him all the kingdoms of the world and their splendor.

"All this I will give you," he said, *"if you will bow down and worship me."*

Jesus said to him, *"Away from me, Satan! For it is written: 'Worship the Lord your God, and serve him only."*

Then the devil left him, and angels came and attended him".

(Matthew 4:1-11)

Let us take a more careful and closer look at what just happened. First, the enemy found Jesus at his weakest point physically during his fast as he hungered. Then he questioned Jesus as the Son of God by challenging him to turn stone into bread and break his fast. The enemy used the phrase, "IF YOU ARE" attempting to provoke Jesus's self-pride. Jesus was strong in the spirit as he was fasting and knew the scriptures. He fought back by answering him with a verse that turns him away the first time. The second time, the enemy approaches The Lord, he uses scripture to tempt him to test God the father by referencing Psalm 91: 11-12, but Jesus knowing the scriptures well, partially recited the verse:

"YOU shall not tempt the LORD your God as you tempted Him in Massah."
(Deuteronomy 6:16)

On the last attempt before he fled, the enemy revealed his true intention: he would give him all the riches of the world if only Jesus would bow down and worship the enemy as God. Jesus never bowed as he answered Him, to God only He will worship.

Did you realize how the enemy can even use the scriptures and manipulate the truth? He will also come to you at your weakest point and attack you through self-pride. But we also know from the Bible if you resist the enemy, he will flee. The best defense is to know the word of God, this will keep you from getting manipulated and played like a fiddle.

Although the scriptures and prayer are just some of the things you must be equipped with, another is fasting. This is equally important. You must understand that when we fast and deny our flesh, we strengthen our spirit man. In addition, food makes us sluggish and clouds our minds, especially unhealthy foods and meat. Bringing yourself to a state that denies your flesh and focusing on God, strengthens your spirit man and you actually become more effective with prayer and hearing God.

When I fast, I abstain from all foods or anything that has calories and only consume water or coffee and tea without any condiments. You can choose to fast any way that you're comfortable with; some of you may not be able to fast for 24 hours or at all due to health conditions. You can choose to do a partial day fast or abstain from something else that you crave daily. Pray righteously, do not sin, and expect God to give you His ear. Try to isolate yourself with the Spirit in a quiet place if you can, so you can hear God when you're in deep prayer. To fast effectively is to stop recognizing yourself with the matters of this world and your human needs. Prayer and fasting establish cohesion and unity. Jesus himself said that some demons can only be cast out with fasting.

Don't keep a clean house empty! The scriptures tell us that when you cast out evil, evil will return with more evil spirits. You must cast out the wicked and ask the Holy Spirit to come in and take hold of the person, area, or house that you are spiritually cleansing. If you don't, then you are better off without the cleansing, hence the saying "the devil you know, is better than the one you don't". I will reiterate this point again: always ask the Holy Spirit to come in and occupy the newly cleansed space. I actually developed the habit of asking God to cleanse the area I'm in and mute the ears of the enemy before I begin prayer. I ask God to come down with Holy Ghost fire and consume all demonic spirits that linger around me. I then ask for the Holy Spirit to fill the space and deliver my message to God's ears only. This is an example of what I do personally, because I noticed a pattern of praying for things and the opposite would happen for a little while. It felt intentional and manipulative; it was a strange and uneasy feeling. One day I was with the Deacon from my church and he just decided to tell me to pray quietly in my mind so the enemy doesn't hear what I say. This lit up a light bulb in my head, and I was completely taken as I remembered all the times I was attacked and didn't even know it. I felt hijacked. That's when the strategy changed. Remember, we must think like soldiers, because we fight spiritual warfare everyday whether we realize it or not.

Salvation! Know that through your faith and belief that Jesus died for your sins and rose from the dead on the third day, you have been saved. God is looking and listening to you through your Savior Jesus Christ. He is blameless, unlike us, and that's what gives us access to a Just God. You have been redeemed from the sins of your past after you have repented and confessed your sins. Your righteousness is of Jesus's righteousness and you are the inheritance of the Lord. After you repent, do not live in the past. If God can forgive you then you should be able to forgive yourself; your standards cannot be higher than God's. Please don't confuse this for conviction after doing something wrong. God will always convict us and nudge us back in line because He loves us and doesn't want us to perish. I am specifically talking about not forgiving yourself on matters you have repented from before God. The enemy loves to use guilt to keep you dwelling in the past to constantly convict you, this is a form of access to attack your mind and soul.

Let us discuss frequency for a moment. This should give you an idea of how everything in the physical can affect the spiritual. Frequency is also called the "language of God" and understanding that everything you can see, say, think of and touch emits a certain vibration called frequency. This is measured by a universal system of units called Hertz (Hz). Frequency is the rate at which current changes direction per second, one Hz is equal to one cycle (current or voltage) -- in other words, this is a measure of energy moving. Now that we are just as knowledgeable in frequency as Heinrich Hertz, the German physicist who discovered it, we can talk about how this is relative.

Remember a time when a person, could have even be a stranger, walked into a room you were in and you immediately, either loved or hated them. Without ever saying a word to each other, you felt a certain level of comfort/discomfort with them. Sometimes we make lifelong friends instantly and the contrary to this is true. We all have or had one of these friends; the one who's always miserable and hates everything about their life. They complain about everything under the sun and tend to make you feel so depressed as they bring about this negative energy within their presence. The saying "misery loves company" has a deeper meaning now. Then there is the other friend who seems to be lucky everywhere they go, they are funny, charismatic, and put the biggest smile on your face every time you're with them.

Why does this happen you ask? Because our vibrations and energy either mesh with one another or they don't; their vibes affect us in either a positive or negative way. Frequency doesn't just stop here; for example, the earth releases a frequency of 7.83 hz. Everything else you can think of, including your words and the things you dwell on, emit a frequency. You vibrate a certain frequency so your words and the energy that's behind it can change things in your life or the lives of others.

*"DEATH and life are in the power of the tongue: and they that love it shall eat the fruit thereof. "(**Proverbs 18:21**)*

Think about that the next time you fall into the whirlpool of a "Negative Nancy" (nothing against the name Nancy, just sounded good together), or talk about matters that don't build but destroy, cursing and speaking bad things about yourself or others. We must be alert in this matter, because people and things can and will bring about certain energies that could or could not be favorable.

Let me give you an example of this energy that is attached to things because of a wicked tongue that cursed it. One late evening I decided to go online and buy an antique picture of our Lord Jesus. I kept browsing until I found the St. Veronica Handkerchief painting of Jesus Christ.

This is a painting by Gabriel von Max who was an Austrian artist born in 1840. I was intrigued by this painting; his eyes seemed to open and close depending on how you looked at it. To be honest, my wife thought it looked real creepy and argued with me about putting it up -- a part of me felt the same. The face of Jesus looked dark and sort of an evil imitation of him. I blew it off and thought it's a unique painting of Jesus and I shouldn't feel guilty for hanging it up. A month went by and the energy in the house started to change. I started to argue with my wife frequently and things felt out of place. There was this uneasy feeling in my home and I couldn't figure it out. I prayed always and asked God for his peace and protection, but this eerie feeling just didn't go away.

One night before I went out for my jog, I got into it with my wife pretty bad before I went storming out of the house. I started running towards the park just a few streets over. I made my way to the swing set, as I needed a place to sit. Then I called the Trinity Broadcasting Network's prayer hotline that I have reached out to for years. As soon as the kind yet enthusiastic voice answered the phone, I was eager to cut him off and explain why I needed prayer. I swear I will never forget how he then quickly cut me off from talking and told me that I have something in my house that's breaking my hedge of protection! Then he asked if I had brought anything in my home recently? My body filled with goosebumps everywhere and I immediately thought of that painting. The man prayed for me over the phone before he hung up.

I started searching for information on the artist on my phone's web browser. I continued the rest of the way home, all while thinking *how did he know about the item I brought into my house.* I made it to my front door step still staring at my phone, reading an old article on von Max. My breath was taken away as I discovered he was into the occult and communing with the dead, and that he incorporated that ideology into his art. I quickly knew what to do as I went to the backyard and threw a log into the fire pit and lit it up. I then went inside and grabbed the portrait off the wall and took it out of its frame. I threw the glass out in the garbage, after shattering it, and then I made my way to the flames that were waiting to consume the evil thing in my hands. I threw the wooden frame into the fire first and let it burn before I tossed the picture in. I will never forget what happened next: As God is my witness, this portrait, which was a photocopy of the original painting, sizzled with intense flames, like fire burning within a fire. It was almost like watching a jumping jack firecracker go off. The blaze had a neon green shade to it with very bright orange and red flames that mixed within that volcanic blaze. I knew this thing was possessed after seeing the way it burned. I spent a good portion of the night praying and washing my home and family with the blood of Jesus.

Things went back to normal after that.

Be careful of the things you hold on to and bring into your lives. Watch what you talk about in the presence of others and think about to yourself. Be aware of your company and the people you choose to surround you. Seek God and His word; it will keep you at peace. Put on the full armor of God and always pray with authority and in the spirit. Know you're the child of a King and you have power and dominion over evil. You have been redeemed through Christ. The enemy is more afraid of you becoming educated in this matter. Now is the time to take control over your life and stop being the victim and become the victor. I made that choice with the events that took place in my life; I refused to accept the loss.

CHAPTER 2

-Keys To The Prison Door

I'm in a prison cell and my sister is also in the same cell with me. I'm look-ing at her and am taken by her beauty. Her hair was curly and vibrant. Her makeup was flawless; she was wearing jeans that fit impeccably, and a blue blouse. Her stilettos where shiny and made the perfect clicking sound every time she took a step. She walked in style, with swagger, even though we were locked in this prison cell. As I was looking for an escape, I noticed the keys to the cell hanging on a hook not too far from my reach. I stretched my arm out as far as I could until I was able to pull the keys off the hook with my fingertips. Finally, I was able to grasp the keys in my hand, and as I quickly retracted my arm closer to my body, I eagerly drove the key into the keyhole and opened the door. I grabbed my sister's right hand and we walked out of the cell and off into a green pasture.

I WOKE UP FEELING GOOD about the dream. However, I was exhausted and nervous because I didn't understand why I was in the prison cell with her. I knew my 28-year-old sister was going to recover from leukemia, even though, at that time, she really didn't look like she was doing that well. I took the dream as a sign to keep praying for her recovery. (She was being treated at Westchester Medical Center at the time.) Nonetheless, I held on to my newfound deepening of faith.

Six months prior to this dream, when we found out about her diagnosis, my family was shocked beyond what our minds could believe. She was complaining of severe headaches before she went to the emergency room, and had the cancer diagnosed from running bloodwork. The next day she followed up with her primary doctor for more blood work to confirm the emergency room's findings. My brother called me up frantically, as he was leaving my sister and her husband behind at the doctor's office. He broke the news to me that the doctor insisted we immediately take her to WMC for leukemia treatment. My entire family was nervously waiting for the results. Hence, my brother eagerly went with them to her follow up.

He took off ahead of them and drove to my parents' house before they got there. He needed to be alone and take in the devastating diagnosis. When he called me up, I was just up the road at a repair shop getting a wheel alignment on my car. Luckily the car was just coming off the lift as I got the news. I quickly drove to my parents' home and walked in on my mom screaming at a picture of Mother Mary holding baby Jesus and shouting, "You lied to me!" My father was sobbing; it was obvious they found out about my sister.

My younger brother finally arrived ahead of my sister and her husband. He stormed in the front door, tearful, and headed straight to his room to cry into his pillow. It was a horrible time and we were scared of losing her, as this disease never struck a family member before. I ran outside to weep in private and yell at God.

In the meantime, my wife called to ask me if we received the diagnosis. Trying to keep myself composed over the phone, I gave her the news. She immediately responded by saying, "she will be ok; I will test for a possible stem cell donor match". She has type O blood and is a universal donor. At the time, none of us really understood what we were talking about and obviously your blood type doesn't qualify you to be a donor for stem cell. But her heart was in the right place and I appreciated the fact that she said it.

I had to pull myself together. Hearing my parents screaming and crying was killing me and I knew they needed strength and hope, not another heartbroken child crying with them. As I was running in and out of the house waiting impatiently for my sister to arrive and calming my parents, thoughts of God's betrayal wouldn't leave my mind. I tried to keep my reasoning in order and not get sucked into anger with God, and I desperately kept myself collected on the outside even though I was chaotic and confused inside.

My sister finally pulled into the driveway. I immediately gave her a hug and grabbed her hand as I guided her to the front seat of my car. Her husband sat in the back and I hopped in the driver's seat and drove anxiously to WMC to get her further treatment. It was a 45-minute drive and the entire time I was encouraging my sister and doing my best to give her hope and guard her heart from fear. It seemed to be working; she was showing amazing strength about her situation. Although she could have been in a state of shock and disbelief, I took her reaction for what it was at the time.

We finally arrived at WMC. The ride felt like it took 45 hours, as a silent sigh of relief was released from my soul while parking my car. After checking my sister into the hospital and going through the logistics of admitting her, my brother-in-law and I stepped outside to get some air. We walked in separate directions, as we needed that moment alone, to take it all in. I found myself on the green off to the side of the hospital, closer to the parking lot. I fell to my knees and cried out to God, grasping the grass under me with two handfuls, and ripping it out of the ground in anger. I remained in that position for about an hour, in frustrated yet desperate prayer, until my father and brother arrived.

Nightfall had come; we had been sitting in the waiting room for hours while the emergency room tried to locate a bed for her on the 8th floor, where cancer patients were to be treated. My brother and I stepped outside and away from my dad and brother-in-law to get some fresh air and talk for a bit in private. We headed closer to the west wing of the building near the small parking lot dedicated to the emergency room. There, I saw a green cargo van parked immediately next to my car. Then it got strange: there was a handwritten phrase written on the back windows of that van. In big and bold letters, which seemed to be written in a white marker, it read "GODS IN CONTROL" [sic]. I looked at my brother and pointed out the phrase on the back of the van. We then looked at each other and thought, *is it a sign from God?*

Up until this moment I was in a "honeymoon" stage with God, as I had been newly reacquainted with Him for about a year. I grew up a Christian but never followed Jesus as I should have. I was very sinful in nature like most people. Roughly one year prior to this day, I was questioning my faith and I remember being hesitant to dig deeper. I was afraid of finding out a new truth and losing what little faith I had at the time. I was reluctant in searching God for a while, as I was comfortable in my ignorance. Then one day, I decided to seek the truth, whether it altered my belief or not. I pondered, *if God is real, then He will just prove Himself to me, and if He isn't real, then I will know the truth.* Either way,

I had to finally soul search and find out for certain. What do you think happened?

Everything that I researched would point back to a Creator. I'm not going to get into proving God in this book as that's another topic. However, from looking into the parting of the Red Sea, Noah's ark, the existence of Jesus, the Shroud of Turin, human physiology, our solar system; everything I discovered pointed to God. I'll give you a quick example of what I'm talking about:

We can look around and if we pay attention, we can see all the wonderful and beautiful things in nature, God's handiwork. We can look up in the sky at night and have our breath taken away by how magnificent the night sky is, with its distant lights too numerous to count and too far away to visit. We can also think about how complicated a machine our bodies are, and how perfectly the body functions from our mind power, blood circulation, nervous system, digestive system, and so on. If we take an even closer look, we can start to see correlations.

For example, let us think of a microscopic cell, which has several components. It starts with a protoplasm, that is inside a membrane, which has numerous proteins and nucleic acids, all surrounding and drawing energy from a live nucleus. Further, look at the atom, which is likewise a spherical structure that consists of protons, neutrons, and electrons, also around a nucleus. Okay, think about that for a second – now consider the similarities between our tiniest particles and our enormous solar system. It's the exact same design. We have our sun, the nucleus, which holds together and nourishes all of the planets around it, just like the nucleus of a cell, which holds it together and nourishes all the other structures. In my opinion this is no coincidence, rather creation by a creator with a specifically engineered design to make it all work.

In our three-dimensional and logical minds, we will never completely grasp the entirety of God or the universe He has created. We can appreciate and try to learn about all the things God has made. We can learn about God himself so that we can try to do things His way and achieve greater satisfaction with the world we can never understand. Ultimately, it all comes down to faith, which allows us to make that leap from logic and the three-dimensional world into the appreciation of that which we can never fathom.

Up until that day of my sister's diagnosis, I was on cloud-nine and I started to experience God in a new way; I was absolutely obsessed with the topic of God. I stayed up late when everyone was asleep, when the house was nice and quiet, to read the Bible and watch videos of debates, theologians, professors, doctors, physicists, and pastors explaining and teaching abstract concepts of the Creator. I couldn't stop seeking Him or talking about the existence of God. Things looked different, more vibrant, colorful and meaningful. I started to see God in everything from the trees outside my window, to the birds that nested in it, to the people I interacted with every day. It was a beautiful time of discovery and courtship with the Lord.

I remembered feeling a peace from within, and an excitement from without, whenever I discovered something new. I wanted to share my newfound knowledge with everyone so that they could share my experience. I remember talking to strangers and asking them about who they believed God was. I wanted to defend and prove Jesus to everyone that dared to challenge me. A friend of mine, who I love dearly and who is a believer in Christ, a "seasoned vet" if you will, laughed at me once and told me, jokingly, that I was so new at this. I laugh at it now, but at the time, it kind of ticked me off. Now, looking back at it, I can see what he meant; he was trying to tell me *it's not always going to be this easy*, and, *you haven't been tested yet.*

But now the "honeymoon" was over and I needed to be tested. I would either continue to believe in Him and deepen my roots, or I would lose my very green faith. Believe me, I didn't see it this way at the time. Driving back home from Westchester that night, I felt betrayed and got angry with God for not answering my prayers, but rather allowing famine to strike. I pounded on my steering wheel with frustration. When I finally got home late that night, exhausted, I jumped into bed and hoped that I would wake up the next day and all of this would have just been a bad dream.

Sure enough, I woke up and it wasn't a nightmare; instead, it was my family's new reality. However, the strangest thing occurred within me; I hungered for God with more intensity that morning. I woke up praying and seeking Him in a different way. I was more interested in God's healing, His instructions to His children, and the Holy Spirit. I no longer cared to search for whether or not He was real -- I knew He was! This entire time, I was angry with God, not in disbelief of Him.

Remember, it *is* okay to be upset with God and even wrestle with Him at times. This is also a form of acknowledgment of His very existence and the power He has over a situation. Think of it this way: Have you ever argued with a parent and even become upset with them when they didn't do something you wanted? Then, later on in your life, or even after you had children of your own, you'd realize the "method to the madness" that was imposed on you and the lesson it taught. I don't think you believed your parents didn't love you or they weren't your real father or mother; rather you got angry and argued with them to prove your point or express your feelings to them, from the position of your comprehension at that time.

God treated me like that angry child and took the only route that would work for me and teach me. He knew in order to evolve me in my walk of faith, He would have to turn up the intensity and reveal Himself to me in ways that I couldn't just search and read about. He wanted me to experience Him in ways which His existence could never be questioned. He had to bring me to a point of weakness and despair, where He would be the only help that could turn the tide. He needed to tear down the old in me, in order to build me anew. God wanted to teach me things about Himself and inscribe them deep within my core. I had to get "baptized under fire". After all, I did ask Him to reveal Himself to me a year earlier.

During phase one of my trial, God was moving in ways I didn't necessarily see or understand at the time. This is when I began to fast, while I learned what needed to be done when praying over a situation or for someone that was troubled by a stubborn spirit within the spiritual realm. So I started to fast without really understanding the deeper meaning behind it, I just did this out of blind faith. Blind faith is important; this is when your obedience is inspired by a truth you hold within you regardless of whether it makes sense to you, or logically aligns to the thinking of people around you. The Bible talks about having childlike faith; even God recognized the blind faith that children have. Faith that is absolute to them and enough to believe anything a parent says to them.

"HE called a little child to him, and placed the child among
them. And he said: "Truly I tell you, unless you change and become like
little children, you will never enter the kingdom of heaven. Therefore,
whoever takes the lowly position of this child is the greatest in the king-
*dom of heaven." (**Matthew 18:2-4**)*

Children are one of God's most precious gifts and absolutely adorable with their gullibility. They will almost believe anything you tell them. This is not done out of stupidity; a child will believe their parent about anything because they trust and love them. My children believed Santa Claus actually came down our chimney. They were sure that he ate the cookies and drank the milk, after leaving them a bag full of toys under the Christmas tree. Why? Because I told them so. What did I do as a father? I rewarded that belief by putting a bag full of toys under the tree and ate the cookies. The point here is that our Heavenly Father will reward our blind faith in Him, as He sees us placing our trust in Him.

When I tell you the intensity was brought up a notch, I wasn't kidding. My sister's recovery wasn't as smooth sailing as you might think, just because I was praying and fasting for her. I was trying everything desperately to fight in the spirit realm. I even went to her house one evening, since she was back and forth from the hospital regularly; and that night she was at home. I walked into her apartment and knocked on her bedroom door as I pushed it open. There she laid helpless and bloated nearly three times her normal body weight from the massive amount of steroids that she was taking. I couldn't even recognize her, she looked like a different person filled with water, with no hair and her facial features nearly disappearing into a ball with eyes. Her doctor at WMC performed the stem cell transplant that she got from my brother. My brother was a ten out of ten match and a miracle from God, having had such a strong match as a sibling donor.

She developed "grafts versus host disease" post the stem cell transplant, which is something that could happen even with a perfectly matched donor. This is when her body was rejecting the transplant and not knowing what to do, they loaded her up with an insane 80 mg. of steroids, in an attempt to keep her body from rejecting the new stem cells. They were actually planning on bumping her up to 100 mg.

As I sat along her side and asked if I could pray over her, I advised her that it was important to believe and agree with everything I was about to say. I counseled her for a few moments before I began to pray, as I wanted to lift her spirit, re-energize her depleted hope and encourage her with the Word of God. Then, for the first time, I raised my right hand and anointed her forehead with holy oil and began to pray. It was just us in the room as I entered into a trance while praying over her health. I was nervous and shy at first but that all went away after I engaged my faith and relied on the Holy Spirit to help me. It was as if Jesus came into the room and stood over us, helping me pray over my sister.

After what felt like ten minutes, the atmosphere changed in the room, the energy shifted and I was filled with an inexplicable feeling of passion to continue. This encouraged me to press forward more vigorously. Shortly after, my right palm, which was on her forehead, started to get warm and tingly. This warm feeling became a very hot sensation; it was noticeable even to my sister, as she just rested there receiving everything I was praying over her. The heat started to build up more in my hand, as if a hot coal was getting too hot to hold. This lasted roughly 30 minutes or so, before I was finished praying. As soon as I said "Amen", I quickly shifted gears, almost like switching over from an altered state of consciousness back into my normal state. I said to her, "Does your head feel hot? Because my hand feels like it's on fire!" She confirmed the hot spot on her forehead, without really knowing what to make of it. Then I kissed her goodnight, with one last word of encouragement before I left. I don't recall my exact words, because I was still recovering from the intensity of our session. But it was along the lines of, you'll be fine, it'll all work out.

Driving home I was completely intrigued by the experience and more perplexed when 20 minutes later my palm was still hot.

This was a moment I enacted out of faith without question. I followed my intuition as the Holy Spirit led me in this prayer that I had never performed before. I could've used many excuses not to go and pray over my sister. Being shy, feeling foolish, never having laid hands over and prayed for someone before, not knowing how to pray in this manner – these were just some of the reasons not to go over to her apartment that night. But I followed my instinct and was led by the Spirit of God to do just that, and surely, I wasn't alone. He was with me, as Jesus extended His righteous and victorious right hand through me that night.

I experienced God on another level, and it was extremely encouraging to me, as I turned this new chapter with God. I felt like I graduated from elementary school and made it to junior high school.

I felt confident in her recovery after that, as her appearance did not count for much at that moment. It was a matter of time passing, to allow what I knew to be true in my heart, for it to manifest in her physically. That was how I felt at that time; but it was not how my parents saw it. My parents remained anxious about her, as they watched her continue to deteriorate. My sister began to develop brittle bones, as the steroids started to eat through her joints, hips, and shoulders, softening her bone tissue, and making them extremely fragile. This continued to advance for a month from that night of prayer with the hot hand experience. My father's fear for the worst started to take a toll on me, as my nervousness began to build back up again.

My brother-in-law drove my sister down to WMC for what we thought was a routine visit and which we hoped would better improve her condition. Instead, her doctor refused to treat her that day and only offered painkillers. He told her husband to *just take his wife home so she could spend whatever time she had left with her two children and family, because there was nothing else they could do for her.*

My brother-in-law called me up frantically, telling me there was no hope, and that they were getting on the highway to drive back home. I refused to accept what he was saying and a fire roared out of the pit of my stomach. I demanded he take her to Memorial Sloan Kettering Cancer Hospital in New York City, which was another 45-minutes south of WMC.

He was worried about Sloan not accepting her, as it was a private hospital and patients would need a referral from their current physician to get accepted. He explained to me that they tried to get her in there previously and had no success. She had multiple issues between her physician not referring her for treatment there, along with Sloan not taking her insurance plan. I argued that he should take her immediately because they had nothing to lose, and maybe if they entered through the emergency room, they wouldn't refuse treating her. I even called up my cousin, who happened to live 20-minutes from Sloan, to meet them there, to help convince the staff if they refused to admit her. We were desperate and acted in that way. We were willing to try anything, as this was her last chance to get her the medical attention she desperately needed.

The first miracle happened when they arrived at the emergency room. "Name and date of birth please" the triage nurse asked, as my sister was pushed in a wheelchair to the small office that stood aside the ER. Hesitantly, she gave them her information, with the fear of being turned away. My cousin was pondering up a "sophisticated" argument the entire time for their rebuttal. As the nurse was typing her information into the computer, their hearts were pounding in uneasiness as they all were praying under their breath. "Oh there you go, you're under the care of

Dr. Steinburg." My cousin and brother-in-law then found themselves being shoved out of the way as a ten-person team swarmed my sister with IV's, bloodwork, medications, and a thousand questions about her condition. They found themselves shouting the answers over the crowd around my sister, as they were nothing less than shocked and in complete disbelief of what just happened.

My cousin finally called me; obviously, I was impatiently waiting for her call. I was laying back in my recliner with my eyes closed, prayer beads in my hand while in meditation and prayer, when my phone rang. I jolted up like a solider jumping out of bed at 4am to the sound of Reveille.

"Hello, what happened? Did you have to give them your 'sophisticated rebuttal'", I answered.

"Not at all. You're never going to believe what just happened!"

As she was explaining to me what took place in the emergency room, tears of joy started rolling down my face and I thanked God, *in a whisper*, while she went on with excitement. I knew at that moment that my sister will live and God was with us and had not left us. It took this moment to experience God in such a way of divine favor, as her information was entered into the hospital's computer system and assigned to a receiving doctor. Nothing could have explained this moment: we did not know anyone on the inside, her insurance wasn't the right plan for the hospital to accept, and she couldn't get a referral even when her life depended on it. The only explanation is GOD.

This was a time where reality looked very scary. I could have easily accepted what the doctor at WMC told us and brought her home that day for her "remaining time," but I didn't lose hope or faith. I continued to PUSH (Pray Until Something Happens) forward with God. I believed that he wouldn't leave us or forsake us according to His promise. I spoke and acted in absolute faith when I demanded she go to Sloan, as I expected divine favor. This act of faith is the reason she's alive today.

This moment encouraged me to dig even deeper in my faith as God is infinite and you can never know enough. I also understood that God never steps in too late and is able to turn the tide in the blink of an eye. I saw God in an entirely different light. No other situation would have allowed me this experience of divine favor.

The effect of the night with the hot-hand experience never went in vain. The life I spoke over my sister that night moved God in the spiritual realm. The faith I enacted that night paid off. God rewarded my childish faith in Him by answering my prayer in a way that revealed His grace.

CHAPTER 3

-Lifting me up

I'm in a courtyard and I'm standing on the bottom of a two-foot-wide concrete staircase just about the width of my body. It was a very narrow and long stairway. These steps ran alongside a brick wall with no railing on the opposite side facing the open courtyard. Hundreds of pale green demons that looked ill, with no hair and resembling skinny manlike monsters, were inching their way towards me, with the intention of grabbing my leg and pulling me off the steps and into their grip. I started running up the treads and made it roughly one third the way up the staircase before I got really tired and winded. I took a knee because I couldn't continue the climb up anymore. These demons are now uncomfortably close to the reach of my leg. My heart started to pound out of my chest and fear filled my soul. I thought it was over; these demons were inches from grabbing my ankle.

Then, an unexplainable figure appears from nowhere and comes up behind me. He gently puts his arms under my armpits and lifts me to my feet. This man starts to walk me up the steps slowly, creating a bigger distance between the demons and myself. As we near the top of the steps, I look behind me in the hope of getting a glimpse of the unknown figure that brought me to safety. I start to scan this man with my eyes, in slow motion from his feet up, while turning my head and peeking over my left shoulder, before my body could make the complete turn.

I first noticed his brown sandals and perfectly pedicured feet, followed by the bottom of his snow-white robe. As my eyes made it to his waist and the core of his torso, I saw the purple sash draped across his body from his left shoulder. At this point I knew who this figure was and I couldn't bring my head up fast enough to see his face. It was Jesus Christ, and I was very eager to get a glimpse of his appearance. My heart was filled with joy and a sense of relief from the danger I just escaped. My eyes were about his chest and shoulder height now; it was almost torture because it felt like my head was heavy and I was forcing myself to see his face. Every centimeter I moved my head closer to his face felt like an eternity had passed. But when my eyes made it as high as his head, all I saw was Jesus wearing a traditional tallitot. His prayer shawl was white and blue, the colors of the Israeli flag, with the Star of David on it. Finally, His face, the part I've been so excited to see!

I didn't know what to think or expect. Was His image like the depictions I was familiar with? Or did He look completely different from what I expected to see? The fact that I am about to see the Messiah with my own eyes brought about a sense of bliss that couldn't be explained. At last, my eyes have finally arrived to his face! At first I was shocked, then my breathing relaxed and my chest stopped puffing up and down so intensely anymore. I did not see his face! I was so disappointed. Rather, his head was made up of an extremely bright beam of light, an illumination that was pure and transcended peace. Bright enough to light up a football field but wasn't blinding as I looked directly at Him. I couldn't see any of His facial features as His brilliance was too powerful to allow me to see His face. He resembled a radiance of energy in the shape of a man in a robe.

Finally, I'm at the top landing of the staircase in a safe position far away from any evil, as He helped me get to my safe haven after rescuing me.

I OPENED UP MY EYES from my sleep feeling a sense of calmness and peace. As I stretched and made my way out of bed, I thought, "I can't believe I just saw Jesus in my dream". Still groggy, I dragged myself into the kitchen to grab a cup of coffee. I started to tell my wife about this dream I had had, since she was always asking me to interpret her dreams, she did not have much of an explanation for me. She continued to prepare breakfast and didn't say much after her initial intrigue.

Although I was calm about it, I was more so baffled on why he came to visit me in the form of rescuing me. I also thought, why am I not excited after seeing the Lord in my dream? What was the message here? Later on that day, I made it to my parents' house kind of eager to get this vision of the night off my chest. I couldn't stop thinking about it and wanted to tell my mother about this unique dream. As usual, I barged into my parents' house without knocking on the front door, and with a quick hello to my dad who was sitting in his favorite couch, I bee-lined it to the aroma coming out of the kitchen. I sat on the stool in the center island and began to tell my mother what I saw. I shared my dream with her, as she quietly stood there listening, and as my father was also eaves-dropping from the living room. As I waited for her take on the possible meaning, she stared at me with a mystified look, yet intrigued, and she said, "it was a good dream," and continued stirring up her sauce on the stove. I started shaking my head into my hands, frustrated. I swear, I felt like I was seven-years old again!

By this time my sister was doing much better. We found out from her new doctor she realistically had about a week to live when she first arrived to their care. Talk about feeling a sense of relief that she survived, thanks to the Lord. They were still lowering her steroid levels, but her condition was much better than when she first arrived at Sloan just a few months ago. My sister still had a long road ahead of her before a full recovery. It was nice to see her look more like her normal self, though.

Her hair got longer; she was more mobile and didn't use the wheelchair as much. She was still keeping up with intense doctor follow-ups and medical treatment, she was in good hands as the Lord spared her life.

My relationship with God was good and I felt confident in my growth at this point. The Lord continued to work on my faith, as I continued to learn about the Lord's ways and depended on the aide of the All Mighty helper, The Holy Spirit. I was seeking prayer groups and surrounding myself with other believers as I understood the power of prayer, and the effectiveness of two or more who gather, in His name with agreement.

I started to burn holy incense every evening as I prayed, and kept a candle lit in my kitchen all day, every day. I light a new candle as the old one burns out. The idea behind lighting the candle was to give up an offering to God with my prayers, requests and supplications. The concept of burning incense is to allow my prayers to rise to the heavens while the sweet fragrance from the incense smoke rises in the atmosphere. I continue to burn incense and light a candle to this very day because this ritual has become a part of my prayer life. I followed orthodox Christianity practices with this sacrament, as I felt comfortable with it and liked the meaning behind it. Ancient Jews burned incense in the temples as well. Besides, the incense made me feel like I was in church and created a holy presence in my home. This also helped me set the energy in the room for meditation and prayer. This practice of burning incense over a hot coal and lighting a candle would help me let go of the day and mentally cleanse the thoughts of my flesh. It has become habit for me and manifested into part of who I am and what I do before most intense prayer sessions, especially when I cleanse my home and pray for specific family members or anyone who needs prayer.

Before I prayed, I started to notice myself cleaning any clutter that was left behind by my kids. Something about clutter bothered me and I couldn't start my meditation until everything was sorted out in the room. I didn't notice myself doing this until it happened a few times. This made me wonder, and when I searched into the matter, it suddenly made sense:

"FOR if someone does not know how to manage his own household,
*how will he care for God's church?" (**1 Timothy 3:5**)*

Keeping your home and life in order and well managed took on a new understanding as it correlates with the Kingdom. Cleaning the immediate area around me also helped me not become distracted and it left no excuse for diversion. At times, I would find my eyes and mind stray away for a bit and think about the untidiness around me. Random thoughts during prayer would also pop in my mind, especially of concerns from throughout the day. Distractions and negative self-thought can happen during and outside prayer, as they often do. When I notice my mental disruptions start, I take it very personal and serious, as I understand it's an attack on my mind and I need to take immediate action to fight it off. I would war back the spirit of the wandering mind or any other destructive thought by promptly rebuking it, referring to God's Word and ask the Holy Spirit to keep me focused on Him. Then, as the clouds clear in my head, I would resume prayer or whatever I was doing at the time.

Remember, the mind is satan's playground and he will try to infiltrate your thoughts and keep you from focusing on God or anything good. He will put the thoughts of all your problems and anything you lack in the forefront of your consciousness. You will suddenly feel like these problems need your immediate attention for resolution as they cannot wait for later. God will give you thoughts of encouragement and the ability to do the impossible, while the enemy brings in self-doubt to counteract the work of God. The Lord will build you up and the enemy will try to tear you down. In 1965, a Baptist pastor, John R. Bisagno, wrote the book "*The Power of Positive Praying*". He spoke of a missionary who has a black dog and a white dog always fighting inside him, and that the dog which he feeds the most will win. In the same way, feed the good dog, which is the good thought, and you will win! We don't have self-thoughts, its either God or the enemy whispering into your soul. Think of the type of fruit that your thoughts will produce before you give it anymore of your energy.

This is one of the enemy's tactics. Spiritual arrows will be fired at you and camouflaged as your problems, obstacles you're facing, depression, and anything that is missing from you or your life. This will come at you from all angles if you allow it, especially during communion with God. Unless you understand what's happening, it will continue, and your connection with the Lord will always be distorted and ineffective when you unknowingly choose to give the enemy your mind. This is very subtle and feels like it's coming from you and not the enemy. These problematic thoughts will be magnified and carry a sense of dire urgency for your attention. You can effectively change the situation by handing your issues to God. Although this attack can come throughout any point of the day, as it usually does, he especially loves to fire this attack at the convenient moment of spiritual union with God. As I reiterate this point, this form of spiritual attack is to keep you from being effective in your prayer, living a life fulfilled by the promises of God and create a distance between you and your Savior. The further you are from God, the weaker you become and susceptible for more intense attacks, with a resulting loss on your end. This attack, if it gets worse, will begin to take over your mind constantly and become ingrained within your subconscious mind, as it will alter the energy you put out and become part of your paradigm.

Your subconscious is altered when thoughts and feelings occur simultaneously. Next time you daydream about your life, pay attention to your thoughts and the feelings that you're experiencing during that moment. You must be self-aware and make sure the feelings that are attached to your self-thoughts are ones that make you feel good and encouraged. If not, you will emit a frequency that attracts negative energy. This potential whirlpool could suck you in if it becomes more frequent and persistent over time. This phenomenon works both ways. If these thoughts are self-promoting and positive in nature, your projects and outcomes in your life will be favorable for success. Take control of your thoughts as you keep your focus on God in all situations and the success of the outcome you desire. Be aware of the energy you radiate because it all works together, for you or against you.

"KEEP your heart with all diligence, for out of it spring all the issues of life." ***(Proverbs 4:23)***

This is a form of how the spiritual realm coincides with the physical world. To fight this on your own, like many self-help books teach, will only last so long before you fall back to your familiar patterns of thinking. We are weak and have no stamina without the Holy Spirit. You need the help of Jesus to break the spirit of the wandering mind, self-destruction, depression[3], pessimism, fear, and any other thought that doesn't encourage you. What we dwell on every day becomes a programing code for the subconscious mind. Our subconscious mind is what puts out a frequency that's either favorable to us or not. Keep God in your consciousness always, as you seek His will and His mind in all situations. Knowing His

---

3   If you must be on medication, please do not stop taking it.

word will reprogram your paradigm and give you immediate encouragement. In addition, when you know the word of God, you consequently know the truth. When you know the truth, the lies of the enemy will no longer affect your life. For instance, the Bible tells us not to be afraid a total of 365 times, a daily reminder for the entire year. It also tells us that fear is not from God, God gives us the spirit of sound mind, power, joy and peace. Knowing this as truth, you will not be afraid when you normally would be. Just focus on the day you're in and not tomorrow's problems; God will resolve them for you. Just have faith that He will.

"THEREFORE do not worry about tomorrow, for tomorrow will worry about its own things. Sufficient for the day is its own trouble."
(Matthew 6:34)

"THESE things I have spoken to you, that in me you might have peace. In the world you shall have tribulation: but be of good cheer; I have overcome the world." **(John 16:33)**

The Holy Book tells us to be knowledgeable of all the devices the enemy can use against us so we don't have any excuses. We must not be ignorant of his trickery and deception. You must know the enemy as described: he steals, he lies -- as he's the king of deception -- he destroys, he tempts you, and he ruins every good thing. He is also labeled as a lion ready to ambush you. This is referenced in:

*"BE sober-minded; be watchful. Your adversary the devil prowls around like a roaring lion, seeking someone to devour." **(1 Peter 5:8)***

Be aware of the intentional invitation from the enemy. The eyes and ears are the windows to the soul. Everything you listen to or watch could allow an attack on your spirit. This happens when something ungodly is being poured into your soul, and if your heart agrees with it, even if for just a smidgen of a second, it could open for an evil attack. Keep in mind, from birth we are wicked by nature, so our flesh will naturally gravitate to things that are sinful. Another reason our flesh tends to be sinful is because it requires less energy -- because we are not resisting the devil. But to stand guard over our thoughts and push back against the evil one requires a greater amount of energy. Our flesh will always want to do the least amount of work. So because we do not want to expend the energy to work with God, our unawareness allows the devil to succeed.

The life we live in is spiritual warfare! Your issues are not with people, or bad luck, or unfavorable events; it's with the spirit world behind it. It's been this way from the beginning of time. The Bible's first recorded battle of mankind was spiritual warfare, when Eve was tempted by satan. He got into her mind and manipulated her thoughts. He planted seeds of doubt in her as he tried to make God look foolish by not letting her eat from the tree. He then denied the truthfulness of God's word, representing the knowledge to be gained from the tree. This followed by attacking God as he accused Him of keeping her ignorant while he painted an image of the Creator being selfish. This attack also revealed for the first time "self-pride" in mankind, because Eve felt her lack of knowledge made her inadequate from the lie that planted a seed of ego. After this, sin entered man.

It's been this way from the beginning of time and it will always be the same battles fought. The scriptures are very clear about this and are spelled out in the book of Ephesians:

"FOR we wrestle not against flesh and blood, but against principalities, against powers, against the rulers of the darkness of this world, against spiritual wickedness in high places."
(Ephesians 6:12)

Once we begin to understand the battlefield we are on and recognize Jesus Christ as our Four-Star General to lead us through the good fight, and acknowledge him as Lord and Savior, we become fearless and victorious. God will describe and expose the enemy to us, weaken the enemy for us, while giving us His hedge of protection. He defeats the enemy for us through our obedience and faith in Him. He is the Shepard and we are his sheep. He will guard his sheep as a good Shepard does. Psalm 144 clearly describes this:

> *¹BLESSED be the L*ORD* my Rock,*
> *Who trains my hands for war,*
> *And my fingers for battle—*
> *² My loving kindness and my fortress,*
> *³My high tower and my deliverer,*
> *⁴My shield and the One in whom I take refuge,*
> *Who subdues my people under me.*

> *⁵ L*ORD*, what is man, that You take knowledge of him?*
> *Or the son of man, that You are mindful of him?*
> *⁶ Man is like a breath;*
> *His days are like a passing shadow.*

> *⁷ Bow down Your heavens, O L*ORD*, and come down;*
> *Touch the mountains, and they shall smoke.*
> *⁸ Flash forth lightning and scatter them;*
> *Shoot out Your arrows and destroy them.*

> *⁹ Stretch out Your hand from above;*
> *Rescue me and deliver me out of great waters,*

From the hand of foreigners,
¹⁰ Whose mouth speaks lying words,
And whose right hand is a right hand of falsehood.

¹¹ I will sing a new song to You, O God;
On a harp of ten strings I will sing praises to You,
¹² The One who gives salvation to kings,
Who delivers David His servant
From the deadly sword.

¹³ Rescue me and deliver me from the hand of foreigners,
Whose mouth speaks lying words,
And whose right hand is a right hand of falsehood—
¹⁴ That our sons may be as plants grown up in their youth;
That our daughters may be as pillars,
Sculptured in palace style;
¹⁵ That our barns may be full,
Supplying all kinds of produce;
That our sheep may bring forth thousands
And ten thousands in our fields;
¹⁶ That our oxen may be well laden;
That there be no breaking in or going out;
That there be no outcry in our streets.

[17] Happy are the people who are in such a state;
Happy are the people whose God is the LORD!

We must allow the Holy Spirit to work through us and the art of spiritual warfare will be taught. God will start to reveal things to you, and you will be led by what feels like intuition during battle. This is activated by sincerely seeking and trusting in God. Through Him we can acquire the win over our lives.

CHAPTER 4

-Crow At The Window Sill

I'm standing in a kitchen that wasn't familiar to me, along with two other men. I didn't know them; but they were not there to hurt me. They stood casually over by the kitchen island in the middle of the room as I stood opposite of them closer to the window above the sink. In an instant, a crow perched at the window sill. He looked gnarly with ruffled feathers and emanated an evil intention to harm me. At the sight of him, I became enraged and ran to the drawer in the kitchen island and grabbed a knife. The knife was my mother's that she used for years and refused to get rid of. The knife was old yet sharp and had gray duct tape on the handle keeping the wooden grips sandwiched together. I ran back to the window with determination to find myself and the bird separated by a bug screen which just appeared out of thin air. We looked eye to eye, and as we communicated through our spirits, I said to him, "you will never get what you came for!" With rage

and disappointment, because the crow couldn't enter the kitchen, he extend-
ed his talon through the screen, ripping his claw into the bottom of it. I
immediately chopped off the crow's leg and he flew away hurt.

I WOKE UP TO THE sound of the hospital monitors beeping; I was filled with overwhelming fear and anxiety. I needed a second to register that it was just a bad dream. My blood pressure was surely elevated, as I felt the veins in my neck thumping. I quickly looked over at my four-year-old son to make sure he was okay, as he slept along my side in the emergency room. I then turned my head over to the clock on the wall and it read 2:30am; we had been at the hospital for nearly six hours.

Earlier that night, I had a very worried feeling about him as he was weak and had broken blood vessels all over his chest and stomach. They were the kind that look like those you burst after you've vomited with excessive pressure. I was laying on my living room couch when this strong urge came over me to take him to the hospital. My son was laying on the love seat across from me and looked pale and very ill. Every time I glanced over at him, the urge became more intense, as if there was a silent voice in my head shouting "go now, don't trust the diagnosis of tonsillitis that was made two weeks ago". It was around 9pm when I told my wife I was taking him to the emergency room. She felt just as concerned as me that evening, and for the previous two weeks leading up to that night.

I jumped up off the couch and went out into the fall night to warm up the truck, as my wife got our son dressed. I then grabbed my son and strapped him into his booster seat and then hopped behind the wheel. I backed out of my driveway in a hurry and sped to the hospital. On our way to the emergency room, my son did something very scary. He started to pray to God. I will never forget the words he uttered that night, "Jesus, please heal me." I couldn't believe he just said that. Those words made matters more alarming and I tried so hard to dismiss what he said. Doubt and fear began to quickly enter my thoughts of his condition because of the intuition he had to pray for his own healing at four years old. I chose to dismiss that it could be anything serious, as I wanted my confidence in God to prevail over those fears. Surely, He wouldn't let anything life threatening happen to my son. Still, I had nervous butterflies in the pit of my stomach. At this point, I felt more seasoned than I ever had with God and didn't think I could actually get any closer to Him. He just tested my entire family through my sister's hardship, surely he wouldn't let anything that evil strike us again? Especially to my little boy.

Around 3am, the doctor came into the room with his bloodwork and casually approached the bed where we were laying. "It looks like an infection in his throat," he said, as he started to scribble into his prescription pad an order of antibiotics. I then told him that my son hadn't been feeling well for several weeks and was already on antibiotics. He gave me the prescription anyway, but this time it was for a different variation of the medicine. I requested that his test results be sent over to his primary pediatrician, then I bundled up my boy in his coat and hat and we drove home. I pulled into my driveway close to 3:45am, exhausted, but with a nerve-racking gut feeling about the dream I had in the ER. I opened the back door and undid his seatbelt, so I could carry him to his warm bed.

I don't think I slept much the rest of the night. I had to be up in an hour and half for court, as I had a trial to attend. I was in a legal battle for five years and had finally made it to trial; that morning was the final day of court proceedings. With almost no rest, I awoke from about 15 minutes of total sleep to that aggravating beeping sound from my alarm clock. I opened my eyelids, and immediately noticed that sandpaper feeling on my eyeballs every time I blinked. I knew it was going to be a long day. I forced my way to the shower, as I needed to get dressed and hit the road for about an hour drive to the federal court house in White Plains. As I was putting on my suit and tie, I started to tell my wife about the dream I had in the hospital, and that I was still afraid. She just listened but didn't say much. I completely dismissed that this was a warning dream about my son, and decided that God was trying to tell me something about the jury decision that I should be getting that day.

I got in my SUV and started my drive down to White Plains. The entire drive, I was praying for God's peace and victory over the uneasy feeling I had. I made it to the federal court house by 8am and underwent an hour of the trial before the closing statements were presented. These would leave the jury with their final impression in order to make their decision. We waited for nearly three hours before the jury came back with a verdict. This was the moment that the last five years of my life came to, fate in the hands of twelve strangers. Finally, the judge entered the courtroom with a piece of paper in his hand that read the ruling. He sat down and started by clearing his throat and sipping some water from the glass that had been in front of him all morning. Then he announced the verdict in my favor.

For that very brief moment, I felt joy.

Then, my phone started to ring as I was saying goodbye to my attorneys and thanking them for the fine work they had done. It was my wife and she had terror in her voice. She told me the bloodwork from the ER was received by our son's pediatrician and they wanted to see him right away. I told my wife to take him to his pediatrician immediately and that it would be about 45 minutes before I could get to them. I ran out of the court house like someone was chasing me with a machete. I didn't feel good about this, and began grappling with God about the possible severity of the diagnosis. As I was sprinting across the street to get to my car, the most beautiful and vibrant double rainbow appeared right before my eyes, and the sight of it put me somewhat at ease. I accepted anything that looked like confirmation in that moment of anguish. The entire drive back, I was praying with every ounce of energy that I could drum up from within my soul.

Finally, I pulled into the parking lot and saw my father and brother outside the doctor's office; they had accompanied my wife and son. That made me worry even more. I thought, *what did they know that I didn't? Is it that serious that they drove out to his doctor's appointment?* I didn't know what to think. My face became flushed as I dashed into the waiting room where my wife and son were sitting in anxiety. I sat next to my wife and grabbed my son, putting him on my lap, and we waited to be called by his doctor.

Roughly 10 minutes went by before one of the nurses called his name and brought us to a room in the back, shutting the door behind her as she exited. Now we were waiting for the doctor to come in. A part of me was wishing that she'd never walk into the room, because I didn't want to hear what she had to say about what was wrong with him. When his doctor finally entered the room, she quickly went over to my son and started taking off his shirt to get a closer look at the marks on his body. After a couple of minutes, she started talking about how she thinks it's a disorder called Immune Thrombocytopenic Purpura or ITP for short. This is a low platelet disorder which causes bleeding and would explain the broken vessels that she was analyzing. I didn't believe she was telling me the whole truth. It felt like she was trying to soften the blow and wanted us to hear it from someone else besides her. Having been our pediatrician for many years, this seemed to be as hard for her as it was going to be for us. This uneasy feeling made the experience even more terrifying.

His doctor was adamant that we take him to WMC immediately, to their Pediatric Unit. I almost lost it due to the horrible experience my family had had with this hospital and their doctors who nearly killed my sister. I insisted on Colombia Presbyterian in NYC, as I was more comfortable with that medical facility. However, his pediatrician insisted on going to WMC, so I reluctantly took him there because I didn't want to waste any more time. I said to my wife *let's get him properly diagnosed* and if we needed to transfer him we would.

We arrived at WMC in about 38 minutes, as I drove over the speed limit with no care of getting stopped by the police. We were followed by my dad, brother, and my wife's family who were just as concerned. We quickly checked him in and started the process all over again as we waited for his name to be called. Slowly, other family members started to arrive at the emergency room; there must have been about 20 people between my wife's side and mine. I became more panicked to see everybody there. I knew they felt the worry that I had and that made it more difficult to stay positive and hopeful. I felt they all knew something I didn't, even though we were all waiting for the same thing -- DIAGNOSIS. Don't get me wrong, I love my family and appreciate their support. But in that moment my mind was wrestling in the spiritual realm, and anything that could add fear, did. I felt like my doubts in God's protection were coming to the surface and I began to think of the worst case scenarios.

Several hours had passed and dusk arrived as we remained waiting for his bloodwork to come back from the lab. I paced back and forth in the emergency room mumbling under my breath … outcries to God. Finally, the doctor came back to the room we were in and asked my wife and I to sit down, that she needed to talk to us. My father and brother realized that the doctor was in the room discussing my son's condition and immediately headed over to hear what she had to say.

"I want you to understand that this is totally curable." The doctor said.

My heart sank and a tingly feeling ran through my body as if electricity ran through my entire being. Once I heard that phrase, my heart started to race like never before and my mouth became very dry. I really didn't know what she was going to say next; I couldn't even comprehend a diagnosis as severe as the one she was about to tell us. She gave us the same diagnosis my sister got a year earlier. As soon as I heard the word leukemia come out of her mouth, I lost it completely and in the most rage I ever felt, I punched a hole in the wall above the bed where my son and I sat. What this doctor just told us was my worst fear come true. I started screaming at God. "Again? Really?!" My wife's face drained of its color and she broke down in tears, as she grabbed our son and held him tightly in her arms, barely able to keep herself upright. Due to my commotion, security immediately ran into the room and escorted me outside the hospital. My heart had just been ripped out of my chest, with no mercy, and I felt that killing me would be the least God could do to spare me from this experience.

The police ended up coming to the hospital because of my uproar and took over babysitting me from the hospital security guards outside the ER. There were many people around me trying to calm me down, but everything they said went on deaf ears because my attention was to God. I completely ignored my family and the police officers who were trying to calm me down. With tears in my eyes, directed towards the Heavens, I argued with God. I never felt so disappointed in Him, I kept shouting:

"Haven't I done everything you wanted me to do...

"Haven't I been obedient to you...

"I changed my life for you and put my trust in you...

"This is how you reward me...

"You could have stopped this...

"Why?...

"Just tell me why did you allow this to happen? ...

"Wasn't my sister enough?"

The officers, who had been alarmed, became compassionate; I could tell they were holding back their tears. The female officer almost gave in and broke down; her facial expressions couldn't hide her empathy for me. The male officer kept his hands on my shoulders, trying to remain professional and not hug me, saying anything he could think of that would help me. The officers' entire demeanor changed from when they first arrived, after hearing me cry out to God. They went from warning me that I could be arrested, to trying to comfort me. They felt sympathetic to the agonizing pain that I felt. In the middle of my outcry, one of the registered nurses, who happened to be a Jewish man wearing a yamaka, came to talk to me and the officers. He told us that they were not pressing charges for the damaged wall and that they understood what I was going through. He said it would be okay and everything will work itself out. I offered to pay for the wall but he refused and let me go back to my newest reality.

In the midst of this hurt and anger, my father hugged me and was crying on my shoulder. He was squeezing me with the most compassionate hug he had ever given me. He was the only person there that night who knew the exact pain I was going through. I could never forget that moment of love that he gave me, for he was the only person that stood out to me from the crowd. Throughout my dad's hug, I continued to shout at God for what felt like the ultimate betrayal.

In a flash, an overwhelming feeling of peace came upon me during this chaos, as if a legion of angels came to my rescue. The Holy Spirit had started to turn up the heat on me ... a baptism under fire. I started to feel His peace in a way I never had before. The feeling was so strange, an almost out-of-body experience. My voice felt like it was being silenced to my ears only; I couldn't hear anything I was saying.

I immediately wrestled with myself after the peace of God came upon me. I started to feel guilt for this new peaceful feeling. My soul was being dragged into a tug-of-war between God and the devil. My humanity began to feel horrible for not being worried about my son anymore, and I questioned whether or not I loved my boy. I felt a good father would be genuinely outraged at that moment and not feel peace. It was as if my worrying and shouting were for no reason, it was as if this wasn't actually happening. At the time I didn't really understand what was taking place, I was super distraught and confused. This internal conflict between my three-dimensional, human thought process and the truth of the spirit realm was turning into an all-out war.

I spent that night in the hospital room next to my wife and son, crying myself to sleep. At 7am, I awoke as if someone threw a cold glass of water on my face. My eyes just opened with no warning, and I felt my blood pressure build as I got up to my feet from the green visitors' couch next to the hospital bed. I quickly looked around to assure myself that I was in the right place and that the night before had actually happened.

My wishful thinking quickly came to a dreadful certainty that I was about to experience one of the worst nightmares a parent can face. I gazed at my wife and son who were still sleeping, and I broke down in tears … quietly. My eyes were so watery, I barely saw anything in front of me as I stumbled out of the room and to the bench just outside the hospital.

There, as I sat by myself, I lost it completely and started to cry uncontrollably, as if I was a child who lost a parent at the park. The scene of a grown man crying in despair, accompanied by agony, isn't a pleasant one to watch. I kept my head tucked between my legs, facing the ground, as I rested my elbows on my knees, so I would not be seen by people walking by. Although I was scared and upset with God, I still had a sense of silent peace that would come upon me every so often.

After an hour, I started walking back to the room with puffy red eyes, wearing the suit from the day before, and looking like I just got hit by a bus. I opened the door slowly because I did not want to wake them out of their sleep. I knew that we had a long day ahead of us since the night before didn't provide any rest. However, they were both awake. With a determined tone, I told my wife, "I'm getting him out of here today and taking him to Memorial Sloan Kettering".

I started the phone calls immediately. The first was to his primary pediatrician demanding that she write up a referral to the physicians at Sloan. I made it a point that my son would NOT get treated at WMC, as I had no confidence in their ability to resolve his issue. They had nearly killed my sister a year ago. Between the going back and forth from his doctor and Sloan, I was able to get the two connected and obtain confirmation from Sloan that they accepted his doctor's referral promptly. They had a room for him available and they were expecting his arrival in a few hours. I immediately took this information to the on-call physician at WMC and informed her that we were transferring my son out of there and over to Sloan, and that she needed to start the paperwork involved right away.

If you thought I was angry before -- when I punched a hole in the wall of the emergency room -- I was beyond angry now. I envisioned myself throwing that doctor -- who started to resemble something demonic trying to stop his transfer out of their death chamber -- out of the window (I didn't actually do it, I just felt like it), when she told me, "since he's a minor, we have to keep him here; I can't administer the transfer."

I replied with a voice that showed no humanity, accompanied by a death stare,

"I will take him out of here with or without your paperwork...

"I refuse to let you or anyone in this hospital treat him...

"What part of *Sloan Kettering is waiting for him* didn't you understand...

"His name is in their system and they have a bed for him...

"So, please, let's not complicate this process...

"My son is not your guinea pig…

"This hospital nearly killed my sister who had the same disease!!!"

She answered, "okay, relax, please have them send over documentation that they're receiving him as a patient and I will administer the transfer."

I'm sure she felt intimidated by me, as I had no limits when it came to my son. I wasn't going to let WMC or that doctor dictate my boy's life or put the hospital's best financial interest on my family's back. I was traumatized by their ethics, and they would have had to restrain me in a cell for the rest of my life with a one-million-man army to keep him under their care.

Without wasting time, I took their fax number and got to work. Within two hours my son was in his booster seat in the back of the SUV and I was zigzagging in and out of traffic on the F.D.R. on our way to Sloan. We looked like a car parade with all the family members who were following us on the highway. They were just as scared as my wife and I were and wanted to support us during this most traumatizing moment of our life.

This was just the beginning of a long road ahead of me. This ordeal was my graduation from junior high school, and I was about to enter high school of the "military" academy of spiritual warfare. The next five years became like boot camp for me as I learned how to truly fight and win.

CHAPTER 5

-Walking On Water

"COME," he said. Then Peter got down out of the boat, walked on the water and came toward Jesus. But when he saw the wind, he was afraid and, beginning to sink, cried out, "Lord, save me!" ***(Matthew 14:29-30)***

SHORTLY AFTER ARRIVING AT SLOAN, I decided to go for a walk. I needed to be alone in my misery. I made my way to the elevator and squeezed myself in and pushed the ground floor button. At the sound of the ding, when the doors slid open, I shoved myself out between the crowd into the main lobby. I exited the hospital and started my walk down East 68th Street, mumbling to God angrily. All sorts of people were passing by me, each in their own world. As I was walking around talking to myself, some people looked at me like I was crazy. Others weren't paying me any mind, with their eyes locked on the path ahead of them, trying to avoid collision with other pedestrians on the congested sidewalk. There were people talking on their phones and chuckling in conversation, while some rode their bikes and scooters on the street just along the sidewalk. Tears were pouring from my eyes yet again, which of course created blurred vision. I started to navigate between people with a concentrated effort not to bump anyone. There wasn't a destination I was headed for; I just wanted to escape the 12th floor of Memorial Sloan Kettering and have a little time to myself. My son was in good hands, with very competent doctors working him up, and the entire family was with him too.

I was so hurt and confused by God. "He doesn't exist!" I said to myself, then quickly became angry with Him again. I wanted to turn my back on Him the same way I felt He had turned His back on me. I couldn't believe that I was in that predicament; I trusted God to protect us from famine like this and guard us from it striking again after my sister's suffering. I continued walking, when I saw a church with its doors open, I stopped in front of it and thought *I have something to say to everyone attending that mass.* I marched in and headed to the very first pew. I distracted everyone in attendance with the sound of my dress shoes pounding against the marble floor. I stepped before the female pastor, who was standing in front of the alter. I got her attention in the middle of her sermon and loudly asked if I could have her microphone for a second -- there was something important that I needed to say to those attending service. She signaled me to wait; obviously she didn't want to be interrupted. She probably thought I was out of my mind and my appearance didn't help much either. I was still wearing the same suit that was beyond wrinkled and my shirt was hanging out of my pants, barely tucked in. My eyes were red as wine, my hair was a complete mess, and the 5 o'clock shadow of my beard was more like 7 o'clock. I literally looked like I just rolled out of bed, like I had a rough night out with the boys culminating in a severe hangover that I wished was the case. While waiting for the mic, I started plotting in my head a very short speech containing my premeditated attack on God. I wanted to tell everyone there that God was useless because I trusted Him and got hurt. I wanted them to know that they were wasting their time and should just go home.

The pastor never gave me the mic, and I wasn't going to wait more than five minutes and listen to any more of what she was talking about. I shook my head in repulsion and walked out of there. I continued my way down E. 68th before turning left at First Avenue. My thoughts were being attacked by every single fiery arrow that the enemy could throw at me. It was working! I was fighting with Jesus over His betrayal and His lies to me. I became angrier at the site of strangers laughing in the street -- why are they able to feel happiness and I wasn't.

Their joy was unfair to me! I was the only one in distress in the midst of the crowd. Nothing mattered to me. Now, years later, I know the enemy was rejoicing at my misery.

I kept walking for another 15 minutes before I arrived at St. John Nepomucene Church located at the corner of First Ave. and E. 66th. I stood outside the building gazing at its historic appearance and briefly wondered about the men who built it and the people it served over the last hundred years. By this time, I had burned myself out and I became very tired and weary. I needed rest for my soul, as the enemy just had a field day with me, making me doubt God, giving me thoughts of unfaithfulness, instilling fear in my heart at the highest level, victimizing me, and also making me feel like I was alone and without God.

The doors to the church were pegged open by a small levered steel leg, and the inside was hardly visible. I was squinting from the bright sun trying to see if people were in there for mass or if it was open for the public. My heart tugged at me to enter this building, and a small sense of peace started to come over me again like the night before. I decided to just go in, after all I was tired and needed a quiet place away from the crowded street to sit and be alone.

I walked up a few steps and inside to find candles lit in the foyer just outside the entrance to the church. Once inside, you could tell that this place was built in the early 1900s. There was a beautiful hand-painted mural on the high ceiling inside an overly large dome. The painting, which appeared to be of Jesus, did not resemble many of the pictures that I was used to seeing of Christ. This image was of a man with long gray hair and a lengthy grayish beard. Between his arms, that were spread open, was a white dove symbolic of the Holy Spirit, with its wings also spread just beneath his chest. Underneath the white dove were four angels in a worshiping position looking up at God. The background of the artwork on the ceiling was a light blue canvas which accented the beige stone columns wrapped in gold trim running along the pews down both sides of the church. The architectural details were very particular; the church was built with integrity. I walked up to the seat behind the first pew on the left side, passing people who were scattered on benches that lined up on both sides of the aisle. I slid into the pew and rested my arms and forehead on the back of the bench in front of me. I found myself starring at the marble floor and crying all over again. I had nothing to say to God, I just chanted his name in a whisper that lightly echoed throughout the church.

"LIKEWISE the Spirit helps us in our weakness. For we do not know what to pray for as we ought, but the Spirit himself intercedes for us with groaning's too deep for words".
(Romans 8:26)

I kept groaning and chanting "Jesus" until a puddle of my tears accumulated under me. This went on for nearly a half hour. I couldn't stop weeping and chanting. When I felt my eyes couldn't produce anymore tears, I sat in silence in the same position for a little while longer, before getting up to head back to the hospital. On my way out, just as I made it into the foyer and in front of the grand doors, a man approached me. He had been listening to me cry by myself for a while. He asked me what was wrong, with a strong sense of sympathy? I answered him with two words "my son," as I broke down again in tears. He gently put his hand on my shoulder and told me in two words "Trust God." I then told him goodbye and walked back to my family.

*"FOR the Lamb in the midst of the throne will be their shepherd, and he will guide them to springs of living water, and God will wipe away every tear from their eyes". **(Revelation 7:17)***

*"YOU number my wanderings; put my tears in your bottle. Are they not in your book?" **(Psalm 56:8)***

I started to march back with some peace and a sense of security from God. I felt more confident in the battle ahead of me after I just let my heart pour out before the Almighty. A burst of energy filled me and slowly began to lead me to deepen my roots of faith and trust in God. I made it back into the hospital room and headed over to my son, sat next to him, and started fighting back harder than I ever had. Blocking anyone pessimistic or who showed me extreme worry when talking about my boy, was the first tactic I engaged on that day of October 7, 2014.

My family started to head back to their homes; they live an hour and half north and were also extremely tired from the long day they endured with us. I wished them all well as my wife and I remained behind to care for our son. That night, I started to lay hands on him and speak life over his situation. I completely switched gears from earlier in the day and decided not to give up on God or my family. Besides, this renewing of my spirit was entirely supernatural; I flipped a complete 180° since I left Saint John's Church. There isn't anything else to attribute this renewal of mind and spirit to but God. That night God gave me rest, as I slept through the night like a baby lying in that hospital bed next to my child -- without a single dreadful thought.

The next morning, I woke up with more confidence over the situation. The more I trusted God, the more I was strengthened through His Spirit during this process of my son's recovery. God was my only chance in this situation and I knew this because there were a lot of other children in that hospital who weren't doing very well. Their circumstances broke my heart and drew me closer to God, the safest place I knew.

*"FOR though we walk in the flesh, we are not waging war according to the flesh. For the weapons of our warfare are not of the flesh but have divine power to destroy strongholds. We destroy arguments and every lofty opinion raised against the knowledge of God, and take every thought captive to obey Christ," **2 Corinthians 10:3-5.***

The school of spiritual warfare had just begun to really teach me how to fight since it was my son's life that was on the line! I know this sounds cruel, but you need to remember only the most dramatic circumstances, within moments of despair, will reveal God in ways that would otherwise make it impossible to see Him.

The moments that He could be genuinely sought.

The moments that you could never discredit Him from the favor that you're getting.

The moments of answered prayers.

The moments that you will never forget.

The moments where He was the only way to get through the battle.

The moments where He has your undivided attention because He wants to reveal Himself to you.

These are the moments that God teaches you how to fight while never leaving or forsaking you.

First, I set my mind on God all over again. He was on my mind every single moment I was awake. I couldn't stop thinking about Him. In Psalm 91, the first verse reads:

"FOR he who dwells in the secret place of the most-high shall abide under the shadow of the Almighty."

I didn't know this Psalm at that moment, but God was introducing the first tactical lesson to win this type of warfare. The spirit of God was working, without me even realizing. An interesting fact about Psalm 91 is that early Hebrews used to recite this Psalm seven times a day for protection. Now, I pray this entire Psalm every day, and it's part of my memory bank during any moment I need to reference it. If our minds become trained to focus on God, we then can properly differentiate the logical world we exist in, from the spiritual realm that is within it. God works outside of this three dimensional world, which is perceived as reality in our eyes. To see God, you need to engage your spiritual eyes, then what you were once blind to becomes visible. We must detach ourselves from what we think is reality, and understand that what happens in the physical realm must first take place in the spiritual realm. In my case, I asked God a year earlier to show Himself to me. Little did I understand that I wouldn't actually see His face, rather I would witness Him working on my life through my new spiritual eyes.

The first miracle to happen was when one of the team members treating my son thought they saw something on his brain. My wife called me, as I was in upstate New York working on a renovation project on a house that I was going to sell. She sounded really worried on the phone. I told her not to worry and I would come down there and switch with her. I wanted to spend the night praying over him before his CAT scan scheduled for the next day.

In the morning, I put my son on my lap and we rode down to the radiology suite in a wheelchair. There, they took him away from me, and instead of letting me sit there and wait, I had to go back to the room until the test was complete. Pacing that empty hospital room, in spite of the Orthodox chants that I played on my phone to calm myself, and the prayers I kept up, I got very nervous. In my loneliness and uncertainty, the enemy snuck in and tried to work on me. But I just prayed harder. An hour later, my son was wheeled back to the room, still groggy from the anesthesia as I carried him back to his bed. I asked the nurse how it went, and she said the doctor would be in shortly to discuss the results. So I sat and prayed some more and focused on God's promise that can't be broken.

When the doctor did arrive, he opened the door and with a smile he said, "Mr. Nesheiwat, your son's brain is just as normal as mine and yours, if not even a little better." I smiled and thanked Jesus for the win. My son was doing well and didn't need a transplant and was handling the chemotherapy very well. He suffered a little loss of appetite, but other than that, he was full of energy for the most part. I knew the Holy Spirit was within him; other parents were admiring his post-chemo physical strength. This was the moment I spoke to them about the power of God.

The second lesson of war that was taught was to fast and pray for my son. I started to not eat for 24 hours, and at other times I would stretch my fast out for 48 hours, while I prayed constantly throughout those days. I fasted more frequently every week. I became familiar with the fact that some demons can only be cast out through fasting along with prayer. Fasting is also a way of putting your request for urgency to God as you display obedience in your faith by denying yourself for Him.

One night I called a buddy of mine who happened to be a devout Christian. This guy really turned his life around and travels the world to help and minister to children and adults in need. I asked him to come to the hospital and pray over my son, if it wasn't too much trouble. He showed up in a couple of hours with a friend. It was 9pm and visiting hours were over, so they got denied access by the glass doors just off the elevator before entering the 12th floor. This was very strange as they never denied anyone that visited before, even after hours. That was the only time the nurse working the door did such a thing. This really ticked me off because I knew that was the enemy working against this prayer session. My buddy could see my frustration from across the hall, so he continued to press until he convinced her into letting them visit for five minutes.

Finally, back in the room with my son, my friend, his guest (who became a good buddy of mine after that night) and I were chatting past the hellos, getting better acquainted with each other, and them with my son. The patient's father on the other side of the curtain had been complaining all night about the noise my son and I were making, because he was working from his laptop. We weren't trying to be rude, we were just having fun and clowning around to stay positive. But when my buddy arrived, this man and his son fell asleep. No matter how loud we were, they didn't wake up to the talking and chuckling coming from our side of the drapes. God had put them in a deep slumber, for what was about to take place needed to happen.

This prayer and anointing was ordained by God and part of the plan. Eric and Mike started to pray over my son and Mike, my new friend, poured holy oil over his head for anointing. A few hours into this divine meeting, I realized the two men from the dream of *"The Crow On The Window Sill"* were these guys right here in the room with us. As this revelation was given to me, I became immediately filled with the Spirit of God. As Mike and Eric learned about my dream and revelation, they began to rejoice in God even more.

The five-minute visit lasted five-hours. When God wants to make something happen, there isn't a force in the universe that can stop it.

I was strong at times, mainly when I was with my son. But when I switched with my wife and went back home for work and some rest away from the hospital, I would find myself struggling with fear. My other two kids stayed half the time with my in-laws and the other half with my parents, and I temporarily moved into my parents' house since they didn't want me being alone in my apartment. However, my apartment was the only place I had privacy to cry out to God without being disturbed. I would spend hours alone there before heading back to my parents' house for the night. I would light a candle, burn incense and get on my knees pleading to Christ. I wouldn't stop until I was filled with goosebumps and a renewed inner peace. I prayed persistently and would block out every negative thought about the situation. I refused to believe or accept anything but a complete healing!

I developed a habit of anointing my son every time I was with him at the hospital. A family member out of Florida had given me some blessed holy oil on a piece of cotton which was soaked with myrrh. The story is that a statue of Jesus was seeping this oil and they thought of my son. They collected some of this oil onto this piece of cotton and mailed it to me. After a month of rubbing it over my son's head and body, the cotton became very dry and worn out. I decided to put it away in a small metal container that was 2 inches long by 2 inches wide and about 5/8-inch thick -- the lid popped open and pivoted off tiny hinges. Upon opening the container, there was a mirror on the inside of the lid and three small compartments. It was the perfect storage place for the old but blessed piece of cotton. I placed this container in the top drawer of the night-stand next to my bed, along the side I slept on when I was home.

A month went by, and I forgot I placed it in there. When I would go home for a shower and a change of clothes before heading back to my parents' for the night, I would always get dressed alongside my bed and near that nightstand. I would get uncontrollable goosebumps every time

I came near that drawer. I didn't understand why until my son came home for the first time between his treatments.

That night was an emotional rollercoaster. My boy came home, and at the same time, my daughter developed extreme pain in her abdomen to the point my wife had to rush her to the local emergency room. I thought, "Lord, why can't we get some rest? My son comes home and now my daughter is in the hospital."

An hour later my wife called and said they couldn't figure out what was wrong with my daughter and that they wanted to transfer her down to WMC. I agreed and told her that when my sister returned from her night class, I would have her babysit so I could come down and stay with them. I hung up with her and called my sister to tell her the situation. She told me that it would be half an hour before she would arrive at my apartment. I started to get a bag of clothes ready for my wife and daughter, along with some hygiene products.

While I was getting their stuff together, I noticed a bottle of oil on the dresser that I brought back with my son's belongings from the hospital. I got more oil after that cotton completely dried up because I didn't want to stop anointing him. This bottle was about a third full. I held it in my hands and thought *I don't want to bring it down with me and waste it.* I wanted to save the oil for my son who really needed it. So I started contemplating on what to do. Then I remembered the dry piece of cotton that was hidden in the container in the drawer next to my bed.

I quickly ran to the drawer to soak the cotton with oil from the bottle I had. I was torn and I wanted to also anoint and pray over my daughter when I saw her as well.

I opened the drawer, grabbed the tin box, popped the lid open and saw my very first manifestation of God unfold right before my eyes. The box was seeping oil from the mirror and the cotton was drenched with it. I was in complete shock and couldn't believe what was happening right before my eyes. I grabbed the cotton and it felt like it was sitting in a cup of oil for weeks. I looked closely at the mirror and it was sweating oil. I never poured the oil from the bottle over the cotton, as it continued to stay soaked for about six months afterward. I anointed my daughter and entire family with this blessed oil, and my daughter quickly recovered from an issue that turned out to be truly insignificant.

My faith had been strengthened after witnessing this miracle and my prayers deepened and the fasting continued. I was getting better with trusting God because I remained focused on Him and His Word. At least I thought that was the case, until I reached my *Peter walking on water* moment.

In the Bible, there is a story of Peter and the other apostles who sailed out to sea in order to meet Jesus. As they are waiting for His arrival, they spot a figure walking on water. They thought it was a ghost at first until this man became close enough for them to realize it was Jesus. Peter was amazed at the sight of Jesus. The Lord saw this and directed Peter to come out onto the water and walk to him. Without hesitation Peter followed the command and walked out with his mind set on Christ. Halfway through, Peter realized he was walking on water, just as a storm started to brew. This is not logical and doesn't make sense, he started to think, and he allowed his heart to fill with the fear of sinking just before he fell under -- followed by Jesus pulling him back up.

I was at a follow-up appointment with my son at Sloan. In between treatments, they let us bring him home as soon as his immune system and blood counts recovered after chemo. This was a nice sense of normalcy during the time we waited for the next treatment. It would give us a break from the hospital environment, which was not the most pleasant. During this visit, I was approached by one of the donor team members. This was a doctor who specifically worked on getting patients ready for their stem cell transplant and finding a matching donor for them. She approached me as I was playing with my son in the big game room at the children's waiting section.

"Hello Mr. Nesheiwat, I just want a few minutes to talk to you about your son's transplant," the doctor says.

"Transplant? What are you talking about? I was told he didn't need one. Why the change in procedure now?" I respond.

"I'm not sure what you're talking about. I was never informed of this. I have to call his primary doctor and verify what you're telling me."

The room began to spin, and I quickly uttered,

"I'm getting dizzy…I'm about to faint."

"Mr. Nesheiwat are you okay?"

"I don't know what's happening to me, I'm starting to get cold sweats really bad…my tongue is getting heavy!"

"Help! Help! I need Help! I think he's having a heart attack… Mr. Nesheiwat please stay with me…Do you know your name…. When were you born? Do you have a history of heart problems? Are you a diabetic? Do you know where you are?" They continued to ask.

"My sah…sah…sah…son where is he?"

"Your son is being taken care of, don't worry about him…please tell me if you have a history of any heart conditions?"

"No."

"Did you eat anything today?"

"No."

"Please keep talking to me Mr. Nesheiwat."

I was swarmed with multiple doctors and nurses as I was being rushed down to the emergency room for an EKG, bloodwork, and IV fluids. Two hours later, and after a bag of fluids and all the testing, I was completely fine as if nothing happened. I was getting very antsy and wanted to get back to my son, because he was upstairs by himself under the care of the nurses. Finally, the ER doctor came into my room with a diagnosis of Vasovagal Syncope, and discharged me. According to Mayo Clinic, this condition is when a part of your nervous system that controls your heart rate and blood pressure overreacts to an emotional trigger. While he was telling me that I would be fine and needed to get something to eat, I quickly got dressed. I grabbed my discharge papers, ripped the sticky pads from the EKG machine off my chest, and rushed upstairs to my son. I was speed walking off the elevator and down the hall, as I approached the playroom where he was being entertained by one of the hospital staff. As soon as I walked into the playroom, I ran over to my son and hugged him tightly. Then the nurse told me that the doctor wanted to talk to me before we headed back home.

"Mr. Nesheiwat, I'm so sorry for the incorrect information that was given to you. You're right!... Your son doesn't need the transplant.... our team member should have checked with me before approaching you".

Boy was I relieved to hear that!

"Thank you doctor... that lady almost gave me a heart attack," I laughed, while the weight of the world was released from my shoulders.

On my way home, I sat in the taxi staring out the window and thinking about what just happened.

- How the enemy just used a doctor and placed misinformation in her mouth to tell me.

- How I was just deceived with a lie?
- How I thought I was strong this entire time, but in actuality it was Jesus who strengthened me.

I couldn't stop thinking about Peter walking on water, just as I was walking through this process of recovery with strength and power the entire time. In a moment, Peter lost sight of Jesus and fell under when he was taken by fear, and in the same way, in a moment I lost sight and believed a lie, as I almost gave myself a heart attack and died of fear. I had to keep my eyes and mind on Christ this entire time in order to continue to walk on water.

April 17, 2015, six months and ten days after we arrived at Memorial Sloan Kettering, we were saying our goodbyes to the fabulous staff that cared for my boy, as he was being sent home, now that his last treatment had been successfully completed. We felt like they had become a part of our family this entire time, caring not just for our son, but for my wife and I as well. My son became the "poster boy" of the hospital since he didn't need the final treatment due to his robust recovery. The Lord spared my son and now that I'm on the other side of the equation, I have seen God from a whole new perspective. I saw Him manifest through unexplainable oil pouring from the mirror of that container. I saw Him reveal Himself through divine meeting of prayer. I saw Him remove a false image on a brain CAT scan. I saw Him reveal the enemy as a liar.

And I saw that I needed to stay focused on only Him so I could walk on water.

These lessons and principles that I have learned must be enforced and not quickly forgotten. Although much was taught to me, there was still some weakness in my fight-game. God used the next four and half years to iron out the kinks and reinforce what I just learned. He needed to see discipline and continued growth in my faith. In the school of spiritual warfare, I just graduated high school and entered college.

CHAPTER 6

-Fear Not

"YOU whom I have taken from the ends of the earth,
And called from its remotest parts
And said to you, 'You are My servant,
I have chosen you and not rejected you.

DO not fear, for I am with you;
Do not anxiously look about you, for I am your God.
I will strengthen you, surely I will help you,
Surely I will uphold you with My righteous right hand."
(Isaiah 41:9-10)

FEAR!!!

This was something that I still struggled with and knew I had to conquer. My fear signaled a certain weakness in my faith; a vulnerability that the enemy was using to exploit and attack me. Although I thought I was hiding it well, my fear was on display for all to see.

My wife and the rest of my family new about my obsession over my son. Although I witnessed miracles and the manifestation of God right before my eyes, for years I still had fear in my heart and the Lord knew I was struggling with it. Fear over my son led me to become overly attached and protective of him. He started to get special treatment and attention over his siblings. If I was under the impression that he was catching a cold or just had the sniffles, I would franticly squeeze him fresh lemons and make him my special homemade lemonade to boost his immune system. I only did it for him and not for my other children. Don't misunderstand me, I love all my children equally and I could never choose one over the other -- I would give myself up for all of them. I was just paranoid about my eldest and keeping him healthy due to his history, and that took priority over the rest. Yes, the Lord delivered him and healed him, but I continued to be overly worried about him. You could say I had some battle wounds that didn't completely heal. The smallest thing could be off and I would stay up all night praying over him, and wrestling with God. I got to the point where I would get an anxiety attack if the idea came for me to travel away from home for a few days. I couldn't leave his side. He continued to sleep next to me for years.

I couldn't even hear or read the word "cancer." I would quickly change the radio station or T.V. channel if an ad was playing about cancer. I wouldn't even say "cancer" as I referenced it as "the C word." I wouldn't entertain any conversations about the subject. I even shielded my son from learning anything about it.

One thing I didn't see coming was, when he got older, my son asked me what happened to him. A part of me was always hoping that he would forget and that God would wipe it out of his memory. That didn't happen. He remembered everything, even the wall I punched in the emergency room. As the subject would arise, I'd become flustered and uncomfortable and quickly gave him a watered down version of what actually happened. I even lied to him about it. I didn't want him to even think that he actually went through such a life threatening and dramatic experience.

This fear became amplified when he started to have nose bleeds. I began to panic when the nose bleeds happened several days in a row. I would stay up late at night pleading with God to stop them and mend whatever was wrong. My real fear was a relapse. The days when my son would go with my wife to his monthly follow-ups at Sloan, I would have a complete anxiety attack until I got the call that his blood work was okay. I refused to go with him to his follow-up appointments; instead, I had my wife take the trip with our son. I couldn't even go back to the hospital for fear of flashbacks of the events I wanted to so desperately forget.

When I got the phone call from my wife with the good news, I would praise God for His finished work. Before that call, I would ask God to bless me with victorious news. Do you see the problem here? I thanked God for His finished work, but <u>after</u> I got the call <u>confirming</u> His finished work. I should have thanked God for His finished work <u>before</u> I got the call from my wife confirming what I knew to be true deep in my heart. Asking God for a victorious report is fine, however it depends on the context of your prayer. In my case, the Lord gave me my victory a long time ago. It was finished, and I should have been fearless when I asked Him for celebratory news. The problem was that, after all that He had shown and done for me, I still asked in fear.

I always believed, and had faith more than I ever had, but there was this "little fear" which transcended doubt into the spiritual realm. This was hard for me to admit to myself, but that was the truth of the matter. This was the window that the enemy used to attack my mind with deceitful thoughts regarding the worst case scenario, thus creating an illusion of a false reality in order to steal my victory. The enemy wanted to regain territory he'd lost to me, so the weapon of choice for him was FEAR. When these episodes happened, I would erupt with turmoil within my soul. I became restless. I would pray and cry out to God, begging and pleading for a sign of confirmation that everything was alright. I know I am painting a picture of myself that's completely different from the previous chapter, but the fear was something I tried hard to hide although it was very noticeable at times. I was ashamed of it because I went through so much and grew so much in my faith, that I should have been freed from the imprisonment of fear.

As time progressed, the monthly visits became every three months. This was a very good sign, as more confidence grew with the doctors to not check him as often. My anxiety became more at ease with the nose bleeds. I still struggled, but with less paranoia as his follow-ups would have revealed anything of concern. This temporary relief was from his doctor's confirming that he was healthy, not from accepting God's finished work prior to the follow-up. Hence, my fear was a subconscious lack of trust in God. The closer we got to his three-month follow up, I would build up on fear again until I got that phone call.

The three months became every six months, and you would think that I would rejoice in the Lord with complete confidence. I rejoiced in God for sure, but the fear was still there, that lack of trust of which I was unaware. Conquering this was more difficult than I had ever imagined and no matter what I did I couldn't get over it. This is because I was still unaware that my fear was actually a trust issue with God.

The six-month follow-ups became once a year, and certainly I was at ease. However, when that appointment would come around, my heart would start to fill with anxiety all over again. This continued to happen even after the hospital labeled him as their "poster boy". God knew how to remove the fear from me, He also knew I was as stubborn as a bull regarding this weakness. Even though I wanted to lose it, I couldn't shake it off.

I started to become more interested in memorizing certain scriptures by heart. I needed to have very quick access to the word no matter where I was in the world, to familiarize myself with His verses that spoke truth and promises that couldn't be broken. This was how I tried to help myself get over the fear that's been haunting my soul.

One night as my son was sleeping, I made my way to my bedroom where he slept every night, and opened the Bible to Psalm 91. I mentioned earlier that this Psalm was recited seven times a day by the Hebrews for protection. Knowing that fact, I needed to know this entire psalm by recollection so I could recite it at any time no matter what I was doing. I stayed up all night memorizing, line by line, until I could recite the entire Psalm without stumbling over a word or having to revert back to the text.

Psalm 91

¹HE who dwells in the secret place of the Most High
Shall abide under the shadow of the Almighty.
²I will say of the LORD JESUS, *"He is my refuge and my fortress;*
My God, in Him I will trust."

Issa Nesheiwat

³Surely He shall deliver you from the snare of the fowler

And from the perilous pestilence.

⁴He shall cover you with His feathers,

And under His wings you shall take refuge;

His truth shall be your shield and buckler.

⁵You shall not be afraid of the terror by night,

Nor of the arrow that flies by day,

⁶Nor of the pestilence that walks in darkness,

Nor of the destruction that lays waste at noonday.

⁷A thousand may fall at your side,

And ten thousand at your right hand;

But it shall not come near you.

⁸Only with your eyes shall you look,

And see the reward of the wicked.

⁹Because you have made the LORD JESUS, *who is my refuge,*

Even the Most High, your dwelling place,

¹⁰No evil shall befall you,

Nor shall any plague come near your dwelling;

¹¹For He shall give His angels charge over you,

To keep you in all your ways.

¹²In their hands they shall bear you up,

Lest you dash your foot against a stone.
[13] You shall tread upon the lion and the cobra,
The young lion and the serpent you shall trample underfoot.

[14] "Because he has set his love upon Me, therefore I will deliver him;
I will set him on high, because he has known My name JESUS
(PRAYER REQUEST HERE).
[15] He shall call upon Me, and I will answer him;
I will be with him in trouble;
I will deliver him and honor him.
[16] With long life I will satisfy him,
And show him My salvation." (supplemental text supplied)

This is a very powerful prayer of protection and of promise by God. I took it a step further and added a few things to it. In red I added the name JESUS and at the end of verse 14 I would put up my requests and petitions to the Lord, because, in the following verse, he promises to answer you.

Adding this to my arsenal was extremely helpful and the more I understood the Psalm, I would see the instruction of God within it. In the very first verse it clearly states that we must stay in the presence of the Lord to remain protected. Keeping in His presence means being fearless. The only fear we should ever have is the fear of the Lord, which brings

wisdom and understanding. Other than that we should never be terror-
ized by the enemy, especially after God has answered us and set us free.
Fear keeps you out of the secret place of the Most-High, which leaves
you vulnerable. FEAR is a LIAR and it will rob you of your peace, joy,
and the finished work of God. It will also cause physiological changes in
your body that could kill you prematurely. Such was the case with me.
Again, I remind you "do not be afraid" is written 365 times, a reminder
for everyday of the year to be free from the shackles of fear.

Over the years, my anxiety with fear got better, but it was never
entirely overcome, as I never fully trusted God. No matter how hard I
tried to conceal this weakness, God always knew what was in my heart.
Because He loved me first, He had a plan to set me free once and for all.
I didn't see it coming because I was completely unaware of what He was
about to do. A plan that looked evil at first, but worked. A plan that
tied together a lot of loose ends. A plan that would further ignite my
trust in God.

CHAPTER 7

-The passing camel

I'm building what appeared to be a small house in my parent's backyard. I'm framing up the walls to this structure, which is being built just behind the main house where my parents live. It was dusk and my father was standing by my side, as he watched me drive nails into the new walls of this structure. We didn't say anything to each other. I was in the zone, focused on building, with some sort of intent, as my father eagerly awaited the completion. I decided to put the hammer down for a moment and step away from the construction. My father and I walked east of their yard, over by the side of their house, to see what was walking down the road. We looked from the backyard to the road that passed in front of my parent's house. There, we saw a mature camel carrying heavy cargo on its back. This large camel just kept walking past my parents' home and down the road. The camel continued on its path. It didn't look left or right, but kept its head straight as it disappeared into the distance.

I AWOKE NOT KNOWING WHAT to make of this message. I'd never seen a camel in a dream before. I wasn't afraid of an evil attack at the time, because camels weren't known to be evil creatures. Every meaning I found, when searching within biblical references, spoke of wealth, but that didn't add up to the way I felt that morning after the dream. However, something about this camel carrying the heavy cargo on its back left me a bit uneasy. The more I thought about this dream, the more the idea of what camels are known for kept piercing at my soul. Camels are known to walk long distances without water. They are also known for their ability to carry heavy weight for that distance. They are very durable and tamable animals.

I began to worry about my parents, because this camel walked past their home. The thought of an attack on my father's household started to worry me a bit, and I began to pray against that dream over and over. I pleaded God's mercy against this dream, without really knowing for certain what the vision was trying to show me, or if it symbolized hard times with my parents. I was working off of intuition of the sixth sense.

I closely monitored them for any changes in their lives. My parents live about ten minutes away from my house, so I visited them daily. Keeping an eye on them wasn't a big deal for me. My biggest concern was my father, as he is a diabetic and stubborn as can be. My dad has also been smoking since he was a teenager and puffed over a pack a day. He's as old school as it gets and trying to get him to adjust his lifestyle isn't easy. I tell him all the time, "you're not superman anymore ... you need to watch what you eat ... try to get some walking done ... you need the exercise." He would then answer, "I could still beat your ass." I would laugh while thinking to myself, I need to pray and fast harder for him. My mother's health was never a concern for me since she never smoked and was in all around good health. She ran the entire household, doing all the cooking, cleaning, and care-taking of everyone. She watched over her children and grandchildren. She always made sure that she sent us some of her cooking if we couldn't make it there for one of her big meals.

Both my parents are very traditional in the sense of how the household is run. My father and mother are very sweet, although my dad could be more on the rugged side since he grew up a badass and always had that reputation in his younger days. Although he mellowed down as he got older, his alpha would always find a way to reveal itself. He has a big heart made out of pure gold, and if he was concerned for one of his children or grandchildren he would pick up and leave in the middle of the night just to check up on us. Whatever is in his pocket he would hand over to his kids.

My mother also has a heart of gold and would literally wake up out of her sleep to feed us. She gave up so much of herself taking care of us when we were younger. She barely slept because she would stay up late cleaning the house after her young, wake up early to get us ready for school, and make sure there was a hot meal waiting for us when we got home. It wasn't easy raising five children who are roughly two years apart. We didn't make it any easier when we were children because we were very needy, especially me. But she would always have her children, and later her grandchildren, lay their heads on her lap and spend 20 minutes or so praying over us.

I grew up in a tough neighborhood and my dad was on my every move in fear that I would mix with the wrong crowd. He wasn't afraid to discipline us; like I said he is very traditional. This is a lost art today, in my opinion, which is reflected in many modern day children's bad behavior. Mom also has the sixth sense; I mean, she always knew when I was up to no good in my young, bachelor-living-at-home days. My father would be her last resort if I didn't straighten up.

As an adult, I make sure to take care of them. I always do whatever I can to help them out. I deal with all my father's real estate affairs, attending to his tenants and handling any miscellaneous repairs. I manage anything he throws at me to ease the burden of stress on him. I just want him to enjoy his life while I take as much pressure off his shoulders as possible. (All this, and I keep my personal life in order, too.) I always give my father a bit more attention than my mother. I feel he's dealing with more health issues and that creates a softer spot in me.

Both my parents have been through a lot over the last several years dealing with their daughter and grandson. My dad grew all his gray hairs in this time; people always thought he dyed his hair because it was jet-black up until a few years ago. My mother spent endless nights praying and caring for us during our family's turbulent years. She never slowed down, even when she started to get joint and back pain from all the standing and running around the house she does. My parents, to me, are the ultimate caregivers and would give it all up for us at the drop of a dime. They did the best they could to raise us and provide everything we needed.

My parents' protégé is my youngest sister, who just graduated from law school. My dad feels like he accomplished his life goal with her becoming a prosecutor in the District Attorney's Office. I never fulfilled that dream for him and neither did my brother or other two sisters. This is part of the reason the lawyer of the family is spoiled rotten by him. She got away with stuff that the rest of us never would have. She has more of a best-friend relationship with him; she says things to him that would have gotten my head chopped off. But, it's pretty awesome to see him morph into this kind of man, showing a much "softer side".

The oldest of the girls lives in California with her husband and two children. She visits once a year, unless my parents go out to her for a little vacation. She's the most sensitive woman I know; with the most generous heart I have ever seen. She works extremely hard taking care of her children and running a large daycare in which she has ownership. She never misses an occasion to be generous and mails out gifts to my parents along with anything else they need. You can spend hours with her and get lost in conversation because she's the perfect hostess. She is the sweetest of them all.

My middle sister, who was saved by Christ, lives just five minutes down the road from my parents with her husband and their two children. She never seemed to want to leave my parents' side; she spends most of her days at their house, as if she never really moved out. Yes, we make fun of her for that all the time! We actually call her "Killian" after my parents' cat who always sat around on the couch and would only move from one room to another. Jokes aside, she has strength that is beyond this world. Even as a child she was always the alpha out of all my siblings. I can't tell you how many times as kids she beat up my brother. I can't help but laugh at it still today, thinking of him squirming for dear life. She has the strongest mindset of them all; no wonder God chose her for this trial. She is the only one who could survive it. There isn't anything that she wouldn't do for her children and family. She takes after our mom the most, and it shows in her cooking. My other sisters could barely boil an egg, even with instructions out of a cookbook. But she can cook up a storm, to perfection. She, too, has a very compassionate heart with a very mellow personality. But her laugh could wake the neighbors when she gets going. She and my mother are very close, especially since her ordeal many years ago. During that time my mother took care of her, as if she was a baby all over again. That obviously made them closer and more attached than ever before. She holds a very special place in my heart, since I fought for her life with tenacity and persistence - behind closed doors. I would never have accepted losing her. Thank Jesus for His finished work on her.

My brother still lives with my parents and has not settled down as of yet. He rebels more than he probably should and that drives my dad crazy. My father literally wants to get up at times and give my brother an old school beat down when he starts his temper tantrums. Watching that scene unfold is hilarious because my brother will take off, like the wind, when my dad gets angry and ready to chase after him. He is the character of the house and brings all the action to any sit-down. He is super quick with his smart remarks and will have you in stiches laughing once he gets going. He was always a mama's boy growing up, since he is the second to the youngest of the pack. You can say that the lawyer stole his thunder when she was born and still owns that thunder until today. Although he is extremely talkative with an energetic and humorous per-sonality, he keeps his feelings hidden and locked deep inside a vault. Just recently, I discovered he has a vast understanding of plant life and enjoys gardening and landscaping. I never would've thought that he'd be into plants! It caught me off guard, although I certainly don't mind. I made sure he helped me with my landscaping several times. Although he tried to give me every excuse in the book that he was busy, I still made him come and give me a hand. It was fun to watch him work on something I didn't know much about and to see him sweat for once as I watched. Just kidding! I kind of helped him out. On a more serious note, he has a very big heart and is always willing to help in any way he can.

My wife and I have now been married for 11 years and we just had our fourth child not too long ago. My wife spends her days raising our children and making sure that they understand the importance of good hygiene, are responsible, and ensures that they are never left out from anything that they should experience. She's definitely the machine in the house; she can juggle more things than anyone I know. She is like supermom, since she attends to the aide of each child's homework assignments, making sure they are educated, as well as doing the cooking, cleaning and keeping an eye on their individual needs. She, too, is very traditional regarding family values, which is one of the many reasons I married her. Our children are her life and she wouldn't exchange them for the world. Plus, she deals with me and I can be a pain at times - but I make it up to her as often as I can. She's an awesome daughter to her parents and cares for her family with great compassion. She's just as great a daughter-in-law to my parents, never leaving their side and caring for them like they were her own mother and father.

My life is my children and part of the air I breathe and the rhythm that synchronizes my heartbeat. Thank Jesus for them, as I couldn't imagine my life existing otherwise. My eldest is the nerd of the bunch; he spoke his first word before he turned one. He is also very into himself and is discovering the opposite sex; he's always stealing my cologne and slicking his hair with gel before going to school. He's a math wizard and would probably shame many adults in a math contest. He was always fascinated with fossils and the solar system from an extremely young age. Drawing is a hobby that he is very good at, especially lions, and he wins the drawing contest in school every year. His teacher puts his artwork in the schools' hallway for display. He also has the personality to match his pretty-boy looks. There is never a boring conversation with him, as he will humor you and question you to death. Thank our Lord and Savior Jesus for his life, as the fight for my son was a battle that I fought relentlessly and with extreme determination. Fighting for him brought me into a higher level with God. My son made me stronger as a man. I radiate strength today because of what God taught me during that ferocious battle that left me with most of my spiritual wounds.

My princess, my one and only daughter, is as precocious as they come. She has an answer bigger than herself for everything. She catches my wife in traps all the time. My wife hates it because she has to hide her smile from her after every time it happens. She loves to read and has a nurturing personality; she always tries to take care of her youngest brother. She doesn't neglect the other two and will always remember to bring them home their share of ice cream. Her sharp and witty remarks have made her a recruit of my sister, the lawyer. My daughter is very close to her aunt and talks about working with her when she grows up. I actually can't see her <u>not</u> becoming a kick-ass attorney.

My third oldest is the sweetest soul you'll ever meet. He has the biggest heart of them all and would dive in front of anything coming to protect his siblings. He has a very mellow personality, although he can be very funny at times. I don't dare get him mad because it will take me days to make up with him. He is as stubborn as his grandfather. He looks up to his older brother and refuses to sleep in his own bed but instead sleeps next to him. There is a special spot in my heart for him: shortly after he was born, my oldest gave us the scare of a lifetime which kept both my wife and I from giving him the attention he deserved, because we had to take care of his oldest brother. Now, he has the most piercing look of them all; it feels as if he's looking through me at times - mixed with a handsome face and an attitude to match.

My youngest son[4], this one is just plain crazy! He loves music and is the biggest dare dog of them all. He is the "party" in our gatherings because of his colorful personality. He challenges his mom and I every chance he gets. My wife always refers to him as the "sweet and sour patch" and says that he is the "perfect form of birth control" - she swears

---

4   I was lead to his name by God. His name means "My God is Yahweh/YHWH". YHWH is one of many names for God in the Old Testament. I didn't realize the meaning until after I felt I needed that name, so I looked it up.

if she'd had him first, she would have stopped right there. He makes the most adorable faces and repeats everything he hears. He is the perfect blend of both his older brothers. He will climb up anything that is not climbable and will try to get our approval on things he's about to do, knowing it's wrong. I think that's pretty smart for a two year-old; he figures if we say okay, then we can't yell at him about it later. If he doesn't get our approval, he will casually walk away, pretending he didn't hear us, and do it anyway. When he does get yelled at, he will become extremely upset until we make up with him, completely contradicting why he just got in trouble. This is great logic, because it works on us all the time.

At this point, my life is finally in order after many years of spiritual combat. I have accumulated many battle scars from the war I fought for so long. At last, I'm wiser in the Lord and prayer continues to be part of my daily routine, rain or shine, I never cease from it. I continue to fast and anoint my children with holy oil every night. God crosses my mind throughout the day, every day. Any situation I encounter, I immediately place Him in the middle of it as I regard His will in all things. I was spirit-filled and alert to any message that would come to me through dreams or random patterns in the physical realm. I became more and more clever regarding the enemy's schemes and the devices he uses to attack. I developed familiarity with the adversary's rhythm of when he liked to throw his flaming arrows. I even got to the point where I smirked at his petty attack when it came, before I quickly rebuked and pushed him back and away. I recognized that this ability wasn't of my strength, rather it was Jesus Christ and the fire of the Holy Spirit within me that was strong. I was wise to never boast about my strength. I knew God was always standing guard over my loved ones and me. This was my lifestyle; I did all this on auto pilot without thinking about it, or even trying.

The past was behind me and my family and I took the fact that we endured the troubles of the past as trials by God. We always said to ourselves that God tries the ones who love him in order to strengthen their faith. My family was my most important priority after God. I thanked Him for all the members that made up our family, as they are all a very precious gift from God. I felt safe and secure in the Lord and that all our troubles were now behind us. We have grown in faith together and are better people than we ever were.

I became busy investing in my real estate business and started to seek other opportunities for God to guide me through, which He has done with my many dealings in the past. I became overly ambitious in building a future to secure my wife and children financially. There's an old Greek saying, which I paraphrase: "Plant trees so my children can enjoy their shade."

Things have leveled out to normal in my life and with my family. But, there was still something that went uncured? That was my fear of having cancer strike again. The same fear also haunted my father. This wasn't an *in your face, everybody notices,* type of display of fear, rather it was subtle and would reveal itself every now and then. It was a form of attack that never stopped firing at us. In Jesus, one must be set free completely and not be partially imprisoned to anything of the enemy.

CHAPTER 8

-The Vulture That Couldn't Come In

I'm standing in a restaurant alone, surrounded by empty tables and chairs.
The restaurant was wrapped with glass windows overlooking the ocean just
outside. As I stared out the window, a black vulture started flying in from
the distance, at what seemed like light speed. It looked as if it was going to
break through the window to attack me. My heart was pounding harder
with every inch the vulture neared the window. This bird was angry and
aggressive. As he flew up to the window, he stopped in midair, flapping his
wings while floating outside the window, looking at me with a death stare
that was petrifying. I was spine chilled, frozen stiff. I didn't dare to move.
I knew it would provoke him into breaking the window and attacking me.
After a few seconds, he dropped a piece of raw octopus from his mouth and
flew off.

I ran outside, looking up into the sky to see where he went, but he disap-
peared as quickly as he came. I sighed in relief, because he was gone. Then
I immediately picked up the piece of octopus and ran it over to the ocean. I
started to climb down the boulders along the shore, making my way to the
water. I thought, off to the bottom of the sea, as I threw this piece of evil,
raw meat into the ocean with all my might, so the fish of the deep could
consume it.

I turned around and started to make my way up the rocks and back to the
restaurant when, suddenly, it thundered and rain began to pour down on
me. It was as if all hell broke loose from my rejection of this bad omen. I
ran back to avoid this second attack from hell, making it to the front door
as I slipped, fell and quickly jumped to my feet. I finally made my entry
back into the restaurant, locked the door behind me and ran into anoth-
er dining room. It was in the back of the restaurant where there were no
windows. There, I stood and reflected, trying to make sense of what just
happened, terrified by what this demon could possibly want from me.

IT WAS 3AM WHEN I jumped out of bed, frightened out my mind. I was
covered with sweat and I could hear my heartbeat through my chest,
while feeling the pulse in my neck throbbing as it harmonized with the
rhythm of my heart. Still groggy, but trying to make sense of the message
of why on earth this evil spirit would come to me in such a nightmare,

I started to pray immediately. I was absolutely terrified, because the last time a black bird came to me in a dream, I went through hell and back with my son. But that was a crow. This was a black vulture! Vultures are bigger and more wicked than crows! I didn't know what to expect; I knew God promised that my son and sister would never be struck again by this disease. I knew this, as He confirmed it to me many times during prayer and revelation.

I began to worry for my parents, as I remembered the "walking camel" dream that I dreamt a month ago. I started to fast and pray against this vision of the night the following day. I pled with God to fight for me in the spiritual realm and never allow an attempt on my family to happen again. I became quite paranoid and continued to do the only thing that could reverse this attack, pray harder.

Another month went by as I monitored everyone, especially my father, for any changes in their bodies or appearance. I became concerned with my father when he started to develop pain in his toe. He initially refused to get it checked out because he thought he could just walk it off and in a few days it would get better. Days became weeks until, finally, after getting on his case about the discoloration of his toe, he went to see a doctor. He found out that he had an infection and needed to be put on antibiotics immediately. He began the medication and hoped that the pain would disappear sooner than later, since now he was limping pretty bad and couldn't wear shoes anymore. At this point, his doctor didn't really say anything to alarm him about it being serious. The doctor told him that he had a blockage in the artery in his left leg which was slowing down the blood flow to his toe and delaying the healing process. They scheduled him for a same day procedure, within the following two weeks, to open up the blockage. I wasn't really worried since it didn't seem life threatening and it was a very manageable situation.

During this time, my mother started to get really sharp and paralyzing pain in her hip and groin area. The pain wasn't constant at first, and she didn't show any serious symptoms of anything else beside the sporadic shooting pain. My mother slipped and fell a couple of years back and since that fall she had been getting this pain. I felt she definitely twisted something out of whack or pinched a nerve. As the days passed, her pain worsened and she became immobile from it. She saw her doctor and was prescribed pain medication, along with some imaging on the nerves in her leg. I felt that a good chiropractic visit would do the trick and release the pinched nerve. I called my chiropractor and asked him to do a home visit for my mom, as she was in too much pain to travel to him.

My chiropractor arrived at my parents' house an hour or so later, walking in the front door lugging his foldable white table. He used this table, which is more like a foldable bed, for his patients to lie on and get adjusted. He proceeded to unfold the legs to the table and set it in the middle of the living room. While he was setting up, I walked to the bedroom to help my mother to the table, so she could get realigned and hopefully alleviate her pain. That was the first time my chiropractor met my mom, so he started to ask her a bunch of questions, trying to become better acquainted, while attempting to understand her pain and how she hurt herself. After explaining the fall that she had taken years ago and how the pain started since then, he nodded his head in agreement and confirmed she definitely pinched a nerve. He laid her on the table and began to adjust her neck, working his way down the spine and to the hip region. After ten minutes, he was done realigning her back and gently helped her off the table. My mother started to pace back and forth in the living room, with a sense of relief.

"You'll get better the more you move and as the days go by, just don't do any abrupt movements that will put you out of alignment again. You'll be fine; just take some ibuprofen for the inflammation."

After his remarks, I quickly said, "Thanks for coming out Doc. Since you're here, how about I jump on that table for a quick couple of cracks".

"Hop on buddy" he replied.

Man, that adjustment felt good! After hearing my vertebra go pop... pop...pop, I felt all the tension leave my body, not to mention I felt a little taller, since he twisted me like a pretzel. I felt great and my mother was walking around the house; it didn't take her long before she bounced back into rhythm with her normal routine.

A few days went by and ... it was Sunday. I got up that morning like any other Sunday, took a shower and got dressed for church. When church ends, it's usually around 1:30pm and by then the kids are starving, as are my wife and I. This hunger of ours has created a family tradition of dining at a new restaurant after church each week. The kids enjoy it and look forward to trying a different place to have lunch. After we eat, we usually go and visit my in-laws for a few hours and then head over to my parents to visit them as well.

It was roughly 7pm when we arrived at my parents' home, and my mother was in excruciating pain, it was more severe than she had ever felt before. I wasn't alarmed, because I thought it was that damn pinched nerve again. Besides, I cover my family every day in prayer and plead the blood of Jesus over them, so I was not worried about her symptoms. However, my wife felt differently and demanded that my mom get in the car so she could take her to the emergency room. Sure enough, they went and my wife dropped her off at the front door of the hospital. A nurse took her by wheelchair, as she couldn't walk on her own from the pain. My wife couldn't stay with her since the world was under the COVID-19 pandemic quarantine and patients were not allowed any visitors to accompany them.

A few hours went by, so I called the ER to ask about my mother's condition. The nurse told me that she was in a lot of pain and that they were trying to manage it with morphine. She also said that they were doing imaging to try to find the cause of her discomfort. It was now midnight. I called my mother and heard the torture in her voice, as she was barely able to talk to me. At this point, I was getting very frustrated because I wasn't allowed to be with her and the only way I could see her was through FaceTime, but she could hardly lift up her phone for that. I hung up with my mom and called the ER again and demanded to speak to the doctor. I waited a few minutes and, then, a very young-sounding physician answered the phone. I quickly got into a questioning frenzy over my mother and demanded answers. He told me not to worry and that he was taking care of her as if she was his own mother. He further stated that they were doing every test under the sun to figure out her problem. He took my phone number and promised to call me as soon as he had some answers on her condition, regardless of what time of night it was.

I hung up the phone with a heavy and uneasy feeling. I wondered what on earth could cause this pain and couldn't fathom that it was anything serious besides a pinched nerve. I stepped out on my deck, took a seat and I gazed up at the night sky while thinking about my mom and dad. I started to pray while my eyes were locked on the stars in the heavens, and gentle tears began to stream down my face. In the middle of my conversation with God, I saw a shooting star cross the path of my focus. After seeing that, I smiled and thanked God for His confirmation. I felt better and decided to go to bed until I get the call to pick her up.

It was 4am and I was asleep when my phone rang. I quickly awoke, grabbed the phone and answered it. It was the doctor from the ER who I had spoken to earlier in the evening:

"Hello?"

"Hi, Mr. Nesheiwat. I know your sleeping, but I need to talk to you about your mother."

"Yes, is she okay?"

"Well, we did some x-rays on her and couldn't find the cause of her pain, so we went ahead and did some bloodwork on her ... her counts are fine except for her hemoglobin, which is the red blood cells ... it's not at normal levels."

"So what could it be ... her white counts and platelets are normal, right?"

"Yes, those are at normal levels which made me run the test again, and the second time I looked at her neutrophils and, strange enough, that wasn't normal"

"What do you mean her neutrophils aren't normal but her platelets are normal? What are you trying to say?"

"Your mother has leukemia."

"What?!!! NO...NO...NO! That can't be correct. Please test her again!

"I tested her twice to make sure, now I'm transferring her down to Westchester Medical Center. They will be able to further treat her there.... Your mom will be okay; I promise.... Medicine is so advanced today and it'll be fine, I promise.... I need you to pull yourself together.... You need to be strong and you need to give your mom support. You can't do that if you don't pull yourself together. I know it's scary, but I promise you it will be okay."

"O...O...Okay."

I hung up the phone and completely lost it; my wife jumped out of bed, trembling from my crying and yelling.

"What did he say...what's wrong?"

"He said she has leukemia."

I walked out on my deck and became hysterical. I began to shake uncontrollably, crying out to God. My wife was in shock, but trying so hard not to show me her concern. She was trying to calm me down in the midst of her confusion. Thoughts of how I was going to tell my father and the rest of my family began to come rushing in. How on earth was I going to figure out a way to see her? There was no way I was going to let her go through this without having us by her side? I wept with the worst case of shakes and shivers I have ever felt; you could feel the wooden planks on the porch vibrate underfoot from my shaking. When I went back inside, I fell asleep on the couch for a couple of hours. I had just exerted all my energy from shivering and crying.

Early that same morning, I stared at my mom's phone number, wondering what she was going to say about her diagnosis. I also wasn't sure I could keep it together when I heard her voice. Then I thought about calling my brother and sister, but chose to let them at least get a couple hours more sleep before I woke them with the devastating news. I decided to clear my throat and pull myself together. I had to call her and hear her voice.

"Hello mom."

"Hi … I'm Okay, don't worry."

"I know mom, there is nothing to worry about … we have been through this before and it's curable … you know that already."

"I'm not scared; I'll be fine. I feel like they're misdiagnosing me, I don't feel like I have IT!"

"They are not completely sure … but, they are sending you down to WMC to double check, but don't worry about that place, I promise to get you out of there … I love you."

"I love you, too."

I finally broke the news to my brother and sister that morning. They were in obvious disbelief and scared out of their minds. We all had a fair share of confusion about why God was allowing this to happen again.

Later that morning, I picked up my brother and we headed down to WMC for a chance to see my mom and to get confirmation on her diagnosis. We still had some hope that the ER was wrong last night. We arrived at the hospital that we hate so much, and I made my attempts to get a glimpse of her. My brother was completely silent, waiting in my truck. One of the nurses came out, took my information, and said that the doctor would call me with an update as soon as he could. I headed back to the truck and sat there with my brother. We waited a few hours more before my phone rang. I answered, and it was the doctor from WMC confirming she had cancer.

My brother and I wept like little children that day. We both started to yell at God for being so cruel to allow cancer to happen yet again. We wanted to know what there was to prove by this. We didn't understand why, since we had all become God fearing and loving Christians -- more than we had ever been.

We were afraid to tell our dad; we didn't know how to break it to him. The poor guy was going through enough with his toe, which was on the verge of being amputated. Plus, the procedure to open his blockage was in a couple days. We were afraid of his sugar levels going out of control from the stress. This was too much to handle between our mom and our dad. Our world was collapsing fast. My fear over my son had transferred to my mother!

We headed back home and decided to tell dad after his procedure in two days. We pulled into my parents' driveway 45 minutes later to the sight of our father limping out of his car, as he had just pulled in himself from being out. He headed toward us and asked about mom. I started to make up a lie about her condition, since I wanted to stall for a couple of days until his procedure was done. He looked at my brother and I, slightly shook his head in a kind of disbelief, then turned around and started to walk back to the house. That instantly broke our hearts, as we knew he sensed something was wrong. We thought it was harsher to keep it from him, so as we looked at each other, we decided to let him know there and then. I called to my dad, as I followed behind him to the front door. As soon as he turned around and faced me, I almost gave in and cried.

After hearing about his wife, he erupted into tears, even though I gave everything I had to ease the blow and give him hope. We then all went inside for a bit before I decided to go home to sleep some of the stress off. I couldn't leave fast enough. I wanted to be alone. I went home to an empty house; my wife and kids were out. I walked over to the picture of Christ that's hanging in the hallway and screamed at Him at the top of my lungs.

"I can't believe You let this happen again … haven't we been through enough already? … I'm embarrassed to tell people that we're going through this again … this is beyond cruel … my mother … Lord really!!! … what good can come out of this … WHY!!! … answer me … WHY… WHY…WHY?"

I walked to my bedroom and buried myself under my covers, thinking my poor mother was stuck in WMC's death chamber and was going to go through this process alone. As I cried under my blanket, my brother called me with renewed energy within his soul. He told me to come and get him so we could head back to WMC, have mom discharge herself, and take her to another hospital in New York City. I agreed and drove back to my parents' house.

After pulling into their driveway, I hopped in the passenger seat so I could make the phone call to our mom and explain the plan, since she needed to demand her discharge. I also called Sloan and explained the situation. They advised us to bring her to New York-Presbyterian Hospital, which is across the street. Her transfer could be done from there much easier, since they are somewhat interconnected. During this time, my sister called her doctor from Sloan, who she has a really good relationship with, for her help in obtaining a referral for our mother. Unfortunately, we knew what to do since we are all too familiar with the process. Sure enough, my sister's doctor accepted my mom as a patient and entered her into the hospital's system. Things so far were lining up, and my brother and I didn't have time to worry and cry at that moment since we knew we needed to act fast and get her out of WMC.

We pulled up in front of WMC's main lobby and kept the truck running as we waited for our mother to be brought down from that damn 8th floor. When she was finally rolled out in the wheelchair from the elevator, it was as if we hadn't seen her for a year. We rushed to her and started hugging and kissing her as we carried our mom into my truck. She felt a sense of confidence after seeing us and her spirit was renewed. We gave our best attempt to encourage her while driving to NY-Pres.

When we finally arrived at NY-Pres, we brought her in through the ER. She was promptly brought back to one of the rooms and a team of doctors and nurses rushed to care for her. They actually allowed us to go back into the ER room with her, which made my mom and us feel comfortable with the hospital and her situation. I even felt, if she didn't get into Sloan, I wouldn't mind her getting treated at NY-Pres. She stayed there for a week before her paperwork and transfer were approved by Sloan.

This was just the first week of this intense, rollercoaster ride. I felt the weight of the world on my shoulders. The past was now haunting me again and fear over my parents was reaching extremely high levels. I felt fooled this entire time by the enemy. My worry had been for my dad this entire time, yet my mother was the one under major attack. Now I was concerned and scared for both my parents and felt that my sister and son were also vulnerable. I became upset with God, as I was under the impression He promised me that this cancer would never attack us again. I was completely lost and didn't know what to think anymore.

CHAPTER 9

-Sleeping In The Mist

I'm standing in the doorway of my neighbor's house looking into their living room. I didn't actually walk in, I just stood there. Off to the left of the room there was a side door that remained open. Standing there, I could see out that door and noticed a few dogs barking and running towards that side entrance. These dogs were far from friendly and were growling at me. Their fangs were visible as they curled up their lips with a wicked demeanor. They were drooling from the mouth and really angry because they couldn't walk in the door. It was as if an invisible barrier kept them at bay. I became a bit concerned before realizing they weren't able to enter the house to attack me.

I turned my head and looked straight down the house where you could see into the kitchen. There, I saw a pair of friendly golden retrievers, wagging their tails, as they just stood there looking at me. I turned my head back to the side entrance and noticed that the aggressive canines were no longer there. I decided to turn around and leave my neighbor's home, as I wanted to go back to my house just next door.

I began to walk up the street alongside the lawn, because there was no sidewalk. As I approached my house, I noticed it was sitting on top of a small hill, which elevated the property above the main road. There was also a retaining wall that held up this hill. This wall was built extremely well and was strong; it must have been four feet wide and each stone was a large sized boulder that stacked up on top of each other making the wall roughly five feet tall. I walked up the pathway to my house, leading up the few steps that are there, and on to the top landing in front of my door. From the top landing, I turned around and faced the street looking directly in front of my house. I had the perfect view from my higher position. I saw my mother laying on a bed in the middle of the road and my sister sat by her head caring for her; she was stroking her hair in a compassionate manner.

It suddenly started to mist; light rain bringing on a sense of refreshment and peace to us. I felt calm and relaxed as I waved to them the signal to come into my house. My sister then helped our mom off of the bed and walked her up my front steps, making their way into my home.

A WEEK BEFORE I HAD this dream, I was completely broken inside and out over my mom, and I was filled with uncertainty; the biggest question being WHY AGAIN? My mother had been in Sloan for two days and my family and I were eagerly awaiting her bone marrow test results so the doctors could determine which type of leukemia she had. This was important, since it would dictate the type of treatment she would receive. This was a very nerve-racking time, waiting for the results.

My father was completely overcome by fear and depression in a way I have never seen before. He stopped eating, and I literally would have to force him to eat his meals. His diabetes really worried me, as I didn't want him to faint from low sugar levels. To add insult to injury, his toe wasn't getting any better, even after they cut half of it off. His condition was really taking a toll on me, as it was pressure of my father's health versus pressure of my mother's health, stacked on top of each other, and happening simultaneously.

My brother, who was always a mama's boy, was now feeling lost and feared losing his mother. I never saw him pray so hard in my life. Every time I looked at him, I saw the little boy who always clung to her hip and couldn't sleep without her at night.

My sister who was saved by Christ is surely one of the strongest women I know. She, too, was concerned, but held herself together better than the rest of us. She never lost hope! She understood what our mom was going through more than anyone in my family. During this time, she and my wife both took the role of caring for my father and brother, in addition to their children and husbands, and they would both bring a warm meal for them every day without missing a beat.

My wife was my rock. She never stopped encouraging me; she kept me from getting sucked into a very bad downward spiral. She would remind me of everything God has done for me in the past.

My youngest sister was studying for the biggest test of her life, the bar exam (which is a written test), in order to become licensed to practice law. She was torn between being able to stay focused on her studies and worrying about our mother.

My sister who lives in California was completely distraught over mom, since she couldn't travel to NY because of the pandemic. She called us for updates regarding mom's condition, nonstop, throughout the day.

My entire family was emotionally exhausted. My dad continued to pray for his wife and never gave up on God. None of us gave up on God, as we all continued to pray for her recovery. Although we had unanswered questions, we kept our faith.

The day came when my phone rang with a NYC phone number on my caller ID, just as I was pulling into my driveway. I knew it was Sloan; I was eagerly awaiting their call. I couldn't answer the phone fast enough that day. I wanted the confirmation of what type of leukemia she had so they could quickly begin treatment on her. After answering the phone, my jaw dropped in complete disbelief from what the doctor was telling me! He said that the entire test wasn't back yet, and that it would take another day or so. They only had the preliminary results of her bone morrow test. From what they saw, it looked like my mom had two types of leukemia cells growing, which is extremely rare. They said she had Acute Myeloid Leukemia (AML) and Acute Lymphoblastic Leukemia (ALL), and that her chances of survival were about 15% with an aggressive treatment.

I hung up the phone and went into hysterics. The thought of losing her, and her unawareness of the severity of her condition, crushed me even harder. I didn't know what to say to my father and the rest of my family. My wife came running out of the house to the sound of my cries. She asked what was wrong, and when I told her she immediately covered her mouth with both her hands, after she dropped her jaw in absolute shock and disbelief. Realizing her reaction wasn't going to be helpful to me in that moment, she quickly switched her attitude, encouraging me back to my faith. There really wasn't anything else she could have done at that moment.

The entire time that we were outside, I was screaming at God and asking him for a sign that my mother was going to be okay. I demanded over and over to see a white dove land in front of me. That was the only thing I wanted as confirmation. It was a specific request. I wanted the opposite of the black vulture that came to me in that dream.

I didn't tell my father about this new revelation in her diagnosis, as it would have immediately crushed him. My brother, and my sister who was saved by Christ, were the only two besides my wife who knew. My sister who was studying for her bar exam didn't need to know at that moment. Everything she had been working for her entire life was just a few weeks away. My sister in California was kept out of this one for her own sanity; she knew her mom wasn't well but didn't need the extra anxiety since she couldn't travel to see her. For the ones who knew, we questioned God even more now. We asked "why make it this severe with two types?" It kept getting harder and harder to maintain our faith in God. But even though it was difficult, we never quit on Him. We kept believing through all our doubts and questions. We trusted Him to deliver us from this storm as He always had in the past.

The next day at around 8pm, I called the Deacon from our church, because I consider him my spiritual mentor. I have this high regard for him because he gave me my first bible seven years prior, the first bible I ever read in its entirety. He always showed me that he cared, and was deeply sincere. I asked him if I could come to his house, and told him that I wasn't doing very well and I needed to talk to him. He welcomed me to visit his home and waited for my arrival.

When I got to his house, he brought me inside and we both walked into the living room and sat down. He was home alone that night because his wife and children, who are grown, were away. I immediately broke down crying to him, as I was asking, *why again, why so severe this time?* He didn't really have an answer for me, but tried his best to do so with the word of God. He knew I was tired emotionally and spiritually and just needed someone to simply listen to me. The Deacon was aware of the fact that I was pretty well versed in the scriptures and understood that I heard it all before, but continued to give me His word in the chance that something comforting would resonate with me; that it may have slipped my mind. He led me to pray on my own.

That night, sitting in his living room, I wept to God like a child, as I poured my heart out to Him. All the feelings that were boiling up in my chest for the past two weeks just came gushing out as I completely surrendered to God. I continued weeping to the Lord for an hour, the most intense conversation I had with God since the beginning of my mother's diagnosis. It was as intense and sincere as the weeping I did for my son at St. John's Church in NYC nearly seven years ago. When my tears couldn't fall from me anymore, I knew I was done. I got up, thanked the Deacon and went home for the night, as it was nearly 10pm and I was pretty exhausted and needed to sleep.

The next day, I woke up from the dream of *"Sleeping In The Mist."* As soon as I opened my eyes, I felt like a fearless lion. There was a new strength in me that morning; I lost something that had been weakening me for years. A heavy weight was off my chest – finally, I fully trusted God! I didn't FEAR! I could look cancer in the eyes and tell it *you don't scare me anymore!* I felt great about my mother, as all fear about cancer and her condition had been completely removed from my most inner being. I didn't care what the doctor told me about her cancer type. I knew that morning that God had the final say in what happened next. I continued that day in that renewed and liberated mindset. All my stress had vanished after last night's cry out to God, literally vanished overnight. I knew that my help came from the Lord, Maker of Heaven and Earth. Everything I'd been through had now come together, so that the finished work of God could blossom in an instant.

Later that day, I got a call from Sloan – it was my mother's doctor:

"Hello, Mr. Nesheiwat, it's your mom's physician at Memorial Sloan Kettering".

"Yes, hi doctor. Is everything okay?" I casually asked.

"Yes absolutely. I want to give you some good news ... your mother's full bone marrow biopsy has come back and, fortunately, our initial thoughts on her leukemia were wrong ... she just has AML and we will start her treatment tomorrow ... your mom will be okay ... her chances are drastically better then we initially thought."

"Thank you doctor for the good news; I will be down there tomorrow to visit her"

I hung up the phone with the biggest smile and tears of joy running down my face, and I started worshiping God. The devil was a LIAR. He manipulated the situation with inaccuracy to encourage fear and not hope. The doctors are human; the preliminary biopsy report is never the full story and should never be taken as a 100% completed report. We could've lost hope in the very last moments before our breakthrough by allowing fear to consume us.

Shortly after this, my mother went into remission -- after the first day of chemotherapy --and she responded in textbook fashion to the treatment. She even had a robust recovery after all the chemo was complete. My sister, the lawyer, picked her up from Sloan, and brought her home after only one month of being in the hospital. God's divine favor didn't just stop there; my mother has one brother and six sisters all who live overseas, except for one sister who lives here in the United States. They all did the DNA swabs for a stem cell match -- we mailed five test kits overseas and one to my aunt here in America. The one that was a perfect ten out of ten match was her sister who was a few hours away, as God made sure there were no delays for her transplant.

Although my father ended up having his entire toe removed, it was the best thing for him since the infection in his toe could have spread to his leg, which could have resulted in leg amputation. He is doing well now and walking around in his favorite shoes, just like he did before the infection. He, too, was blessed, as it was the third toe (in the middle), which didn't affect his walking at all. Since this occurrence with him, he has been more careful with himself and tries to live a healthier lifestyle than before. My sister who was saved by Christ is doing great and is focused on her family. My eldest son is as vibrant and healthy as any other child his age, and continues to draw everything he can. When God's healing hand touches someone, there isn't a force on earth or beyond it that can reverse it or take it away.

> *"AND suddenly, a woman who had a flow of blood for twelve years came from behind and touched the hem of His garment. For she said to herself, "If only I may touch His garment, I shall be made well." But Jesus turned around, and when He saw her He said, "Be of good cheer, daughter; your faith has made you well." And the woman was made well from that hour."* **(Matthew 9:20-22)**

We had a family friend insist that we test our water -- she works at a water testing facility and offered to do it for us. We took the empty cylinders from her and filled it with tap water from the sinks throughout my parents' house. Several days later she called me up and, as she gave me the results of her findings, I was in shock. My parents' water had three times the level of a chemical called benzene in it. Benzene causes AML, the type that all three -- my mom, sister, and son -- had. After further investigation, it dawned on me that the heating oil tank was buried underground adjacent to the main water line that entered the house.

My mother used the tap water for everything, from washing dishes and cooking, to brewing coffee for the family. We all visited them daily and ate there constantly, and when we didn't come over for a day, my mother would send some of her cooking to our homes. We all have been exposed to benzene for years. Fortunately, it ended the way it did. I removed the oil tank from the ground and installed propane instead. I completely relocated the position of the new tank and rerouted the lines away from the main water feed into the house. Indeed, God revealed to me the source that the enemy used to torture us for so long. What the enemy used for destruction, God used for construction.

The storm always rages the strongest just before your breakthrough; it's the enemy's last attempt to keep you from receiving your miracle, your answered prayer, your only escape to the new beginning that awaits you. The enemy wants you trapped and within his grip, to control you with fear and have you lose all hope in God. The mind is satan's playground! This war has become much clearer now; I saw the lies and deception one too many times. But now I'm free forever.

> *"There is no fear in love; but perfect love casts out fear, because fear involves torment. But he who fears has not been made perfect in love."*
> **(1 John 4:18)**

The FEAR that haunted me for so long is no longer there! I knew with all my heart that my mom was already healed before she started her chemotherapy -- I knew the ending of the story. I am finally liberated because I conquered those thoughts of terror. I just graduated from spiritual warfare college. It took God one last trial of this kind to accomplish what he needed to complete my family's faith and mine, and that was to eliminate fear.

FEAR is also known as *Feelings Equivocating Actual Reality.* These are feelings that pose as real, when they are not; just your perception of what is real. You must face your fears in order to overcome them. Being bound to your fears will shackle you for the rest of your life. I am now truly fearless and filled with hope for tomorrow because I know who my God is today. One who doesn't break a promise and One who will never leave my side or abandon me regardless of how much I wrestle with Him. The Lord promised my sister and son would never be afflicted again, which is a promise He never broke. He never mentioned anyone else in my family. Now, He promised me to never let cancer come upon anyone in my family again and that it is finished.

The day after the call with my mother's doctor, giving me the final results of her bone marrow biopsy, my brother and I drove down to see her at Sloan. That day the Lord gave me the sign I specifically requested a week prior.

My brother was driving and I sat in the passenger seat next to him. Gospel music was playing on the car stereo, and my brother and I felt confidence and joy that could only come from God. In the midst of our conversation, I was looking out the windshield gazing at the trees that we were passing at 75mph. I noticed this brilliant white *thing* off to my right, about 50 yards ahead of our car. The closer we approached this white bird, the more it caught my attention. The brilliance of its white feathers reflected the sun as a mirror would. Before I knew it, my brother started to notice this starkly white bird flapping its wings, as it started to take flight from the tree it was in and head directly towards our car. My brother swerved the car back and forth while pumping the breaks in the middle lane of the highway. His reaction to slow down was because it felt as if we were going to drive into the back of this bird. It purposely chose to skydive to the middle lane, which we were in, and fly in front of us just above our windshield. He yelled at me to quickly grab my phone and record it, but I was too fascinated with this dove and the brilliance it radiated. I didn't dare take my eyes off of it to search for my phone. The dove flew just over our car, about twenty feet ahead of us in the middle lane, and continued to fly over us for about 30 seconds before it sped off and vanished.

In case you didn't know, doves fly at a maximum speed of 55mph. But, we were driving at least 75mph, and even after we slowed down a bit, we quickly resumed speed to tail this beautiful bird. We could barely keep up with it before it took off from in front of us, at what seemed to be jet-like speed, and disappeared into the far distance. This was one of the most amazing things I have ever experienced from God. He took me as I am and answered my very specific request. I smiled and knew in my heart that God just showed me the white dove that I explicitly asked for, when I demanded confirmation a week ago.

CHAPTER 10

-I Shall Not Bow

I was standing along a short wall that stood to about the height of my waistline and was alongside a cliff that was perched high up on a mountain. As I gazed off into the far distance over the cliff that I stood before, I began to see all different types of large predator birds fly in and land on the top of the wall just before me. These birds were not there to harm me and I wasn't afraid of them, rather they were waiting for their leader to arrive. The wall filled with many wicked birds as they flew in and landed one at a time. I stood there and watched them from the distance that I kept.

Finally, after all the minions had taken their positions upon this wall, a huge half-bird, half-man flew in over the perched flock and landed in front of them. He looked like a gargoyle and was very evil. He was definitely in charge and the others were there to simply bow and worship this wicked thing. What I saw was satan and his demons as they all took a bow before him, in worship, with obedience, and fear. They had no power to come near me as I just stood there and watched their ritual with disgust.

The leader of the flock then looked over at me with this evil smirk and gave my oldest son three red roses with abnormally small flowers on their ends. I quickly ran over and snatched the three roses from my son's hand and threw them back at the leader, as I shouted with all my might that we serve and bow to our Lord and Savior Jesus Christ only. I grabbed my son by his hand and fled from them. We ran off and away from their presence as we took refuge in a house. They never tried to chase or follow us.

THE MESSAGE

It's okay to question God. If you're going to intelligently interrogate His existence, then be even wiser to search for Him with an open heart. Unfortunately, I didn't truly accept Him blindly at first, I sought Him and looked for scientific proof before I believed with all my heart. God looks for blind faith like that of a child, they who believe will be blessed beyond measure. The Lord exists in everything that we see in nature and in humanity as His fingerprints are in it.

"JESUS said to him, "Thomas, because you have seen Me, you have believed. Blessed are those who have not seen and yet have believed."
(John 20:29) (Doubting Thomas).

Our spirit is programmed to seek God. From the very beginning of our existence, people from all cultural backgrounds have looked for something higher than themselves. This is no coincidence but is a programmed default within our spirit. Even atheists come to their non-belief in God after seeking him and not finding him. The real question lies with how to find Him. Once we think we've found God, we must make sure we're not bowing before an imposter. Out of all the figures of religion to claim to have the light, Jesus Christ is the only one to claim,

"I am the way, the truth and the life. No one comes to the Father except through me."
(John 14:6)

Out of all the spiritual figures to ever exist, to walk this planet, Jesus Christ is the only one to rise from the dead. The rest have decayed in their graves, just like any other human.

In my case, the closer I drew to God, the more my lifestyle changed to the opposite of what it used to be. I stopped doing all the "little sins" and took a Godlier road with everyone and everything. The enemy didn't like the territory he was losing to me and the attacks began. God used these assaults and turned them into trials to reveal Himself and erase any doubt about His existence from my inner core. The trials became a testimony that "reprogramed" me, if you will, and a new software had to be downloaded within my soul. My battle may be very different from many of you; however, we share a common enemy: the devil.

God is **Love**.

What is **love** you ask? Love is an **intense feeling** of **deep affection**.

What is **intense** you ask? It is extreme **force**, degree, or strength.

What is **force** you ask? It is strength or energy as an attribute of physical action or movement.

What are **feelings** you ask? They are an emotional state or **reaction** thereof.

What are **reactions** you ask? They are an **action** performed by a sensation that's experienced by a feeling or an emotion.

What is **deep affection** you ask? It's a mental state or an emotion that one is in or experiences.

These actions -- which cause a reaction within a state of emotion and give you these experiences -- require energy. **Energy** that moves is a force with a frequency that can be measured.

What is **energy** you ask? According to Britannica, it is the strength and vitality required for sustained physical or mental activity. It's also the process of transfer from one body to another. After it has been transferred, energy is always designated according to its nature. All forms of energy are associated with motion.

How is this relevant you ask? Well, according to Rudolf Julius Emanuel Clausius, a German physicist and mathematician who is considered one of the central founders of thermodynamics, The First Law of Thermodynamics states that energy is always conserved, it **cannot be created or destroyed**. Energy can be converted from one form into another.

God is the energy of love, which was never created and cannot be destroyed and will always be as He Always Has.

"BELOVED, let us love one another, for love is of God; and everyone who loves is born of God and knows God. He who does not love does not know God, for God is love. In this the love of God was manifested toward us, that God has sent His only begotten Son into the world, that we might live through Him. In this is love, not that we loved God, but that He loved us and sent His Son to be the propitiation for our sins. Beloved, if God so loved us, we also ought to love one another."
(1 John 4:7-11)

"I am the Alpha and the Omega," says the Lord God, *"who is and who was and who is to come, the Almighty." (Revelation 1:8)*

My life has been filled with miracles and answered prayers. Perhaps the most important prayer God has answered for me was the one when I asked Him to show me His face. Although I didn't see Him as I expected, He revealed Himself in everything that exists to me. He taught me how to be a better son, father, husband, and brother - a better man. He showed me what blind faith can do for me. He taught me how to fight the battle that matters. He displayed loyalty to me before I gave Him mine. He took me as I am and gave me mercy and grace. He loved me first.

When God taught me how to fight the good fight of faith, He equipped me with the complete armor of God.

"FINALLY, be strong in the Lord and in his mighty power. Put on the full armor of God, so that you can take your stand against the devil's schemes. For our struggle is not against flesh and blood, but against the rulers, against the authorities, against the powers of this dark world and against the spiritual forces of evil in the heavenly realms. Therefore, put on the full armor of God, so that when the day of evil comes, you may be able to stand your ground, and after you have done everything, to stand. **Stand firm then, with the belt of truth buckled around your waist, with the breastplate of righteousness in place, and with your feet fitted with the readiness that comes from the gospel of peace. In addition to all this, take up the shield of**

faith, with which you can extinguish all the flaming arrows of the evil one. Take the helmet of salvation and the sword of the Spirit, which is the word of God. And pray in the Spirit on all occasions with all kinds of prayers and requests. With this in mind, be alert and always keep on praying for all the Lord's people". (Ephesians 6:10-18)

The Belt of Truth

He gave the truth about the enemy, about life, about Him, and anything that contradicts that truth is false. He confirmed His messages to me as truth; I didn't allow fear to give me a false sense of reality based on my feelings.

The Breastplate of Righteousness

He loved me enough to give me Jesus and my righteousness is of His righteousness. This is how I'm justified and not condemned by the enemy.

The Gospel of Peace

He gave me oneness with Him which gave me peace in the midst of the storm within my soul; a bond that cannot be broken.

The Shield of Faith

He took me through a seven-year journey that renewed and strengthened my faith. It was a journey that answered all my questions and gave me strength while removing all my fear. He gave me wisdom to discern truth from falsehood, which shields me from the attacks and lies of the enemy and the world.

The Helmet of Salvation

I trust in Jesus' death and resurrection as the payment for my sin, as my salvation came from a lengthy process of sanctification. I know He was the perfect sacrificial lamb to wash my sins before a Just God.

Sword of the Spirit

He gave me His word to fight with as I trusted and anchored myself on it. As I recited His instructions and promises of all my battles, these same words fought off the enemy with its truth.

For roughly a year and a half before I wrote this book, I kept having the same dreams over and over. I dreamt of looking into a mirror, having photos taken of me, or of someone following me from the shadows with a camera like a paparazzi on my every move. I really never understood what the message meant and kept asking God to give me a clearer vision of what He was trying to tell me.

Then one night, at around 2am, as I was slipping into deep sleep for the night, just before I let go of my wakened state, what felt like a lightning bolt struck my body. I jumped out of bed instantly, gasping for air, knowing I had to write this book for Him. I shook my wife awake. She asked me what was wrong, as she struggled to give me the attention I required from her. I shouted, "Now I have to write the book!!!"

I stayed up for an hour after that realization, just staring at my ceiling. Now those repetitive dreams during the past year made sense; God wanted me to start reflecting on my journey through the past. I began to think of how to begin this message that night. I had attempted to write this book six years earlier but came to a screeching halt after a couple of chapters. But, God was holding me to my promise to Him. Once I understood His curriculum, after graduating from the "Academy", I wrote this book. I now had the full message to share with you. I hope that this book blesses you as it answers some of your questions through my story.

I promise you that, if you trust God with all your heart and all your might, a kind of trust that's without borders, and if you believe with childlike faith and seek Him and learn His instructions, you will be blessed beyond your imagination. He will never leave your side or break a promise, even when it looks like you're alone. What I learned is that the moments when I felt abandoned were the moments He was closest to me. As for my family and I, we will always serve the Lord Jesus.

This book is meant to strengthen the faith of the believer and answer questions for those who have doubt. Pass this along, as it could help the person you least expect. Many people live, in secret or publicly, with countless questions about God. My testimony could be exactly what they need to hear or read for encouragement. This book surely describes the events that unfolded in my life; however, the story is not of me, but of God.

THE END

REFLECTIONS

I ASKED MY ELDEST SON, who was healed by Jesus Christ, to draw me a picture of a lion for this book. A few days later, he came up with this drawing. I initially wanted to put it on the cover; but the more I looked at the sketch, the more I saw my own reflection in it, for many reasons. I then decided to have the Lion of Judah replace this sketch on the front cover. It is Jesus Christ who is The Warrior Within Me and placing Him on the cover is a much more accurate depiction of the Warrior. My son's drawing, which depicts a battle-wounded lion -- whose scars have healed but are not gone, and whose eyes are fixed at the heavens above, looking to God for help -- would be a representation of my appearance from within my soul. An image that no one can physically see of me unless they look at me with their spiritual eyes.

We are all battle wounded warriors; but the difference is, who is the Warrior within you?

A PRAYER FOR THE READER:

I pray that your lives are filled with absolute trust in God, with peace, with joy and with good health for you and your loved ones. I pray that fear never enters your hearts and consumes you. I pray that God guides your path with his truth and goes before you to make the crooked way straight. I pray that my story touches you and brings you closer to God, for we live in very uncertain and deceptive times. I pray that the mercy and grace of God is upon you and your loved ones.

I pray that you accept Jesus Christ as your Lord and Savior, if you haven't.

In Jesus Christ Mighty Name, I seal this prayer over you and your loved ones, Amen

REFERENCES:

Thomas Nelson- New King James Version Holy Bible

Webster-Dictionary

Wikipedia

www.grc.nasa.gov

www.birdsandblooms.com

www.scholarship.org

Encyclopedia Britannica

"*The Power of Positive Praying*" *by* Pastor John R. Bisagno

CPSIA information can be obtained
at www.ICGtesting.com
Printed in the USA
BVHW042141240221
601088BV00017B/353

9 781649 904683